Biofeedback

GRAY
MATTER

GRAY
MATTER

Biofeedback

Krista West

Series Editor
Eric H. Chudler, Ph.D.

CHELSEA HOUSE
PUBLISHERS
An imprint of Infobase Publishing

Biofeedback

Chelsea House
An imprint of Infobase Publishing
132 West 31st Street
New York NY 10001

Library of Congress Cataloging-in-Publication Data

West, Krista.
  Biofeedback / Krista West.
      p. cm.— (Gray matter)
  Includes bibliographical references and index.
  ISBN-13: 978-0-7910-9436-5 (hardcover)
  ISBN-10: 0-7910-9436-7 (hardcover)
  1. Biofeedback training—Juvenile literature. I. Title. II. Series.
  RC489.B53W48 2007
  615.8'51—dc22   2006101019

Chelsea House books are available at special discounts when purchased in bulk quantities for businesses, associations, institutions, or sales promotions. Please call our Special Sales Department in New York at (212) 967-8800 or (800) 322-8755.

You can find Chelsea House on the World Wide Web at http://www.chelseahouse.com

Text and cover design by Terry Mallon

Printed in the United States of America

Bang EJB 10 9 8 7 6 5 4 3 2 1

This book is printed on acid-free paper.

All links and Web addresses were checked and verified to be correct at the time of publication. Because of the dynamic nature of the Web, some addresses and links may have changed since publication and may no longer be valid.

Contents

1 | Biofeedback in Action

The goal of biofeedback is to unite the mind and the body—to make the conscious, thinking mind more aware and more in control of what the body is doing. At its simplest, **biofeedback** is a process that uses instruments to make information about the body available to the mind. The idea is to give the mind the knowledge it needs to heal the body. This, some say, is the key to solving many health problems without drugs or surgical invasions.

Other people seek scientific evidence to support the claims of biofeedback. The science, so far, is incomplete. Biofeedback treatments have been used for nearly 50 years, but formal and controlled scientific studies of the mechanism that makes biofeedback an effective treatment are few and far between. Exactly how and why biofeedback works is still unknown in most cases.

At the same time, there are thousands of emotional, influential, powerful biofeedback success stories out there. Many people claim biofeedback has cured them when modern medicine could not. These claims cannot be supported by hard science, but the following are a handful of true success stories.

JAKE, AGE 8

Jake sits in a dark room playing a video game. The character he controls gobbles dots as it moves across the screen.

There is no noise. There is little visible excitement, and there is no joystick.

Jake is directing the character by altering his **brain wave** patterns. A sensor stuck to his head reads the electrical impulses produced by his **brain** and translates them into directions for the character. Jake thinks relaxing, slow thoughts to move his character in one direction, and he thinks focused, attentive thoughts to move his character in another direction.

Jake suffers from a variety of mind and body conditions, including hyperactivity, **seizures**, and developmental disabilities. He was born three months premature and with severe brain damage. Part of his brain's electrical activity is less predictable than that of most people's.

His story—and his joystick-less video game—is a familiar one to those who know about brain wave biofeedback. Instruments are used to connect the brain to a computer, so that the patient can control the computer with his or her own thoughts. Before beginning his video game treatments, seven-year-old Jake could not tie his shoes, zip his jacket, sleep through the night, or carry on a normal conversation. With daily biofeedback training sessions, his parents began to see near-instant improvements. Today, Jake's brain wave training continues, and he continues to show improvements. Jake can now tie, zip, sleep, talk, and even read.[1]

LILY, AGE 45

Lily begins her session by simply breathing deeply. A sensor strapped to her chest translates her breathing pattern into music. Depending on how she breathes, she hears different combinations of musical notes. She hears the music and knows whether she is breathing as deeply as and she should, and she changes the music by changing her breathing.

Lily is experiencing too much **stress**. She is anxious, unable to focus, and frustrated with how these feelings are affecting her work. She is a professional, successful graphic artist who is no longer feeling artistic. She is frustrated by a temporary inability to think creatively, commonly known as a creative block.

Relaxation biofeedback is helping her fight her condition. After deep-breathing exercises, Lily begins what experts call guided imagery. She imagines being able to create again, designing new and exciting works that earn her the praise of her peers. While she practices these new techniques, temperature and breath monitors give her information about what her body is doing. When the treatment session ends, Lily creates a series of cards that express her thoughts. She uses magazine clippings, paint, and glue to create dozens of imaginative cards. With each treatment session, she feels the creative block slipping away.[2]

BRIAN, AGE 17

Brian sits with a sensor glued to the skin on the left side of his head, right above his ear. The sensor is connected to an instrument that monitors Brian's brain waves. At first, a red light is on. By relaxing his mind and breathing deeply, Brian makes the red light go off and a green light come on. He is learning to change his brain waves with his thoughts. When he changes his brain waves for the better, the green light is his reward. The instrument helps Brian know if he's changing his brain waves in the right way.

When Brian was born, his umbilical cord was wrapped around his neck so that he could not breathe. As soon as doctors delivered him and removed the cord, he started breathing. There was no apparent damage at the time, but when Brian started walking, he began to have problems. He learned slowly and was often angry. When he started school he had trouble making friends and often reported seeing strange colors and shapes. At night, he would jerk violently and sweat in his sleep.

Finally, Brian was diagnosed with **epilepsy**, a disorder that affects electrical activity in the brain. His doctor prescribed multiple medications to treat his seizures but none worked well.

Conditions Treated with Biofeedback

There are dozens of different types of biofeedback treatments, each specialized to target different conditions. Figuring out which conditions can be helped with biofeedback is usually the first step in starting treatment.

The Mayo Clinic, a well-respected medical center and research organization that treats more than a half-million people every year, says that biofeedback has proven to be helpful treating about 150 conditions, including:[*]

- Asthma
- Raynaud's disease (affects blood flow)
- Irritable bowel syndrome
- Hot flashes
- Nausea and vomiting associated with chemotherapy
- Incontinence
- Headaches
- Irregular heartbeats (cardiac arrhythmias)
- High blood pressure
- Epilepsy

[*] Mayo Clinic, "Biofeedback: Using your mind to improve your health," *Complementary and Alternative Medicine*, http://www.mayoclinic.com/health/biofeedback/SA00083 (accessed December 5, 2006).

Some medications made him do strange things like climb onto the roof of his house to light matches. Other medications turned him into a zombie. As a last resort, Brian's parents tried brain wave biofeedback. Within months, his condition improved. He no longer had violent outbursts, and he became more willing to talk. Brian successfully graduated from high school and even started college.[3]

HANS-PETER, AGE 49

Hans-Peter blinks his left eye and the letter *A* appears on the computer screen in front of him. A moment later, he blinks again and an *N* appears on the screen. He sits motionless, watching the cursor on the screen float from letter to letter as he spells a word. Sensors on the top of his head provide the key to what is happening. The sensors read and magnify Hans-Peter's brain waves. These brain waves control the movements of the cursor on the screen. Once his thoughts direct the cursor to the desired letter, a blink of the eye allows him to select that letter and make it appear on the screen.

Hans-Peter has Lou Gehrig's disease, also known as amyotrophic lateral sclerosis (ALS). During the past 15 years, he has slowly been losing control of all the muscles in his body. He cannot walk, talk, eat, or breathe on his own. The only body part he can move is his left eyelid. His mind, including his emotions, intellect, and opinions, is unaffected by the disease. He has a functioning mind trapped in a motionless body.

In this case, the instrument he is using (generally called a computer-brain interface) provides the only way for him and other paralyzed patients to communicate with the world. He is using his brain waves and left eyelid to type his thoughts on a computer. The process is slow, but without it he would have no other way to express himself. Such instruments represent a new generation of biofeedback treatment options.[4]

ED, AGE 50

Ed sits with sensors strapped to his shoulders and lower back. He imagines flying on an airplane safely and happily and focuses on releasing the tension in his back muscles. As he gets deeper and deeper into his thoughts, a monitor shows the tension loosening in his back. As his mind relaxes, his muscles relax, as well.

Ed is afraid of flying, but as a high-ranking executive for a toy manufacturer, he is required to fly frequently for his job. Every time he flies, he gets anxious and his back begins to ache. If the anxiety lasts too long, his irritable bowel syndrome (IBS) flares up. IBS is a disorder involving severe stomach pains associated with changes in bowel movements. These changes can be everything from feeling constipated to having to pass solid wastes too often. The condition is uncomfortable and it can be embarrassing.

Ed is treating his IBS by learning to control his back pain and anxiety with biofeedback treatments. He begins with deep breathing and positive visual imagery and concentrates on relaxing specific muscles in his back. After a few biofeedback treatment sessions, he is able to fly again without triggering his IBS. At the same time, his colleagues comment that his tennis game has been steadily improving. When they ask Ed what he is doing to play better tennis, he smiles and says he has no idea. Ed never reveals that he believes biofeedback has improved his game.[5]

2 | What Is Biofeedback?

At this moment, what is the temperature of your skin in degrees Fahrenheit? Is it 100°F? Is it 75°F? If you are like most people, you probably cannot say the exact temperature of your skin. Your body knows the answer, but this information is not immediately available to your mind.

Place a **thermometer** on your skin, however, and you can quickly read your skin temperature. The instrument makes the information about your body available to your mind. With training, practice, and the visual aid of the thermometer, your mind can learn to control the temperature of your skin.

Using instruments to assist the mind in controlling the body is the basis of biofeedback. The process is difficult to define in a single sentence, but at its simplest biofeedback uses instruments to make information about the body available to the mind. With exercise, the mind can learn to control the body's signals. Biofeedback comes in many forms, but all have these three main parts: signals, instruments, and exercises. To understand how these three parts combine to create the biofeedback process, it helps to start with how the body uses **feedback** to learn.

FEEDBACK

Learning is a skill. We don't think about it very often, but all humans and most animals have the ability to learn. Babies learn how to eat solid foods and walk; young adults learn to read, understand new subjects in school, and drive cars; adults learn new skills on the job. Our minds learn new things all the time without us ever thinking much about how it happens. But how does the mind learn?

Feedback is one process the mind uses to learn. The mind senses a signal, such as temperature or hunger, and replies to the information in that signal. The signal "feeds" the mind. Over time, feedback responses are learned and can happen automatically or through a conscious choice. A shiver is an example of an automatic feedback response. The mind senses a signal, in this case the temperature of the body, and issues a

Examples of Feedback

Feedback is a response to a signal that contains information. Here are some examples of automatic and conscious feedback.

SIGNAL WITH INFORMATION	RESPONSE	TYPE OF FEEDBACK
Cold body temperature	Shiver	Automatic
Hunger pains	Eat food	Conscious
Irritants to the nose	Sneeze	Automatic
Failed exam	Study more	Conscious
Warm computer temperature	Fan turns on in the computer	Automatic
Stock market price	Buy or sell stocks	Conscious

response: a shiver. The shiver helps warm the body with movement and keep the temperature constant. This type of feedback response happens automatically. Eating, on the other hand, is an example of a conscious feedback response. The mind senses a signal, in this case hunger in the form of an empty stomach, and issues a response: to eat. Eating takes away the feelings of hunger. A person's mind consciously decides to get food when the hunger signals arise.

Feedback happens all the time in the human body. It also happens in other places. The stock market, for example, is regulated with feedback. The price of a company's stock is the signal, and the stock traders are the responders. When a stock price goes up, traders might sell the stock to make a profit. When a stock price goes down, buyers will purchase the stock (with the hope of selling at a higher price and making a profit). Earth's climate, windmills, and electronics all use feedback systems to regulate specific characteristics (Figure 2.1). Feedback is everywhere.

BIOFEEDBACK

Biofeedback is a specific type of feedback that trains the mind to respond to new signals (Figures 2.2 and 2.3). The mind already knows how to respond to many signals. For example, the mind directs the body to shiver when it is cold. Other signals are less obvious, such as skin temperature, brain waves, and muscle movements. By learning to read these signals, a person can learn to control a variety of mind and body conditions.

The key is to use instruments that make the body's signals available to the mind. Skin temperature is one example. Your skin maintains a certain day-to-day temperature without your conscious mind contributing much thought to the maintenance process. Add an instrument—the thermometer—and the mind/

Figure 2.1 A windmill uses feedback to keep pointed into the wind. The fantail responds to the direction of the wind by turning the main blades toward the wind, which enables the main blades to spin constantly.

body game changes. For example, a woman sits holding one thermometer in each hand. After much training and practice, the woman can learn to increase the skin temperature of one hand and not the other. She does not know exactly how she

Figure 2.2 A man undergoes biofeedback therapy, a noninvasive, alternative health procedure. The man stares at blocks of colored light while electrodes connected to his head measure different physiological responses such as skin temperature, muscle tension, and brain wave function. Biofeedback is said to help control pulse rate, blood pressure, and migraine headaches, as well as to relax spastic muscles.

does it, but her mind can see that the process is working by reading the thermometers. This is an example of biofeedback in action.

Skin temperature, it turns out, is an indicator of how stressed a person feels. Cold hands result from high stress levels and warm hands result from relaxation. Biofeedback practitioners suggest that learning to control skin temperatures helps a person learn to control stress levels.

Other body signals can indicate factors that affect a person's health. Blood pressure can be an indicator of anxiety, muscle

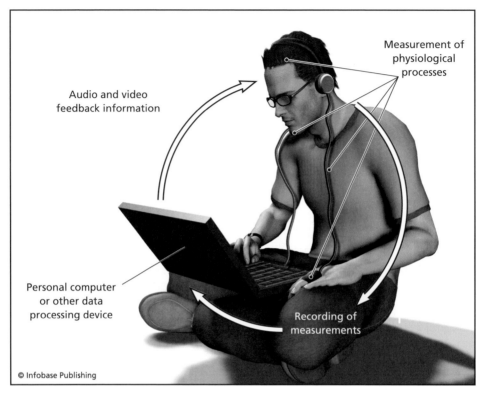

Audio and video
feedback information

Measurement of
physiological
processes

Personal computer
or other data
processing device

Recording of
measurements

© Infobase Publishing

Figure 2.3 An artist's rendition of biofeedback is seen above. In one form of bio-feedback, subjects watch a cursor on a computer screen. At the same time, instruments record brain wave measurements. Those measurements are translated into directions for the computer that make the cursor on the screen move.

movement can be an indicator of body control, and brain waves can be an indicator of a person's ability to concentrate and learn. This book breaks the conditions potentially treated by biofeedback into two basic categories: mental and physical.

Biofeedback: Mental Conditions

Mental conditions, including depression, hyperactivity, and learning disabilities, affect mood and behavior. **Depression** is one of the mental conditions commonly treated with biofeedback.

Depression is a state of extreme sadness or despair that disrupts an individual's daily life. According to Mental Health America, there are about 19 million adults in the United States suffering from depression and related anxiety disorders every year, and as many as 1 in 5 teenagers may suffer from depression.[6] As in all forms of biofeedback, the treatment of depression involves a signal and a response. In this case, the signals are brain waves and the response is a patient's ability to change those brain waves. It is unknown why changing brain waves helps alleviate certain conditions.

Brain waves are simply the electrical signals produced by the brain. To make the information in these signals available to the conscious mind, the patient is connected to an **electroencephalograph** (known as an EEG). Electrodes are placed on the person's scalp to detect electrical signals, and the signals are amplified and displayed on a monitor as brain waves. The exercise comes when a patient learns to change his or her brain waves by watching the EEG monitor and practicing with a trained practitioner. Through various coaching techniques—such as teaching a patient to hold certain images in the mind—the practitioner helps the patient learn to change the brain waves.

With practice, the patient can learn to create brain waves that help relieve depression. For some patients, brain wave biofeedback, often called neurofeedback, works better than traditional medications used to treat depression. (See Chapter 5 for more information on other mental conditions treated with biofeedback.)

Biofeedback: Physical Conditions

Physical conditions are states that affect the senses, muscles, and movement. They might include **incontinence**, headaches, and **paralysis**. One of the physical conditions commonly treated with biofeedback is incontinence, the involuntary excretion of urine through the urethra or involuntary bowel movements through the anus. According to the National Kidney and Urologic Diseases Information Clearinghouse, more than 13 million men and women in the United States experience incontinence. It occurs more often in older people than younger people, and more often in women than in men, but it can affect anyone at any time of life.[7]

Biofeedback from the National Institutes of Health

The National Institutes of Health (NIH) is funded by the government to conduct and support medical research. The NIH is well-known and well-respected by doctors. It defines biofeedback this way:

> Biofeedback is a technique that measures bodily functions, like breathing, heart rate, blood pressure, skin temperature, and muscle tension. By watching these measurements, you can learn how to alter these functions by relaxing or holding pleasant images in your mind.
>
> This teaches you how to control and change these bodily functions. By doing so, you feel more relaxed and may be able to help treat your own high blood pressure, tension and migraine headaches, chronic pain, or urinary incontinence (a few examples of conditions for which biofeedback is particularly helpful).*

* National Institutes of Health, "Biofeedback," *Medline Plus Medical Encyclopedia*, http://www.nlm.nih.gov/medlineplus/ency/article/002241.htm (accessed December 5, 2006).

When using biofeedback to treat incontinence, the signals are muscle movements and the response is the patient's ability to control those movements. To detect muscle movements, a trained practitioner inserts a small sensor into the urethra or anus of the patient. This sensor is connected to an **electromyograph** (EMG), which detects the muscle movements and displays them on a monitor as electrical pulses.

The exercise comes when a patient learns to control the muscle movements through practice. The EMG helps the patient and practitioner know when the exercises are being done correctly. One type of exercise, known as Kegel exercises, or simply Kegels, is named after Arnold Kegel, who first developed them in the 1940s. A patient consciously practices tightening and releasing the muscles that stop and start the flow of urine. At first, the patient and practitioner practice these Kegel exercises together while watching the EMG. Once the patient learns to control these muscles, exercises are performed anywhere from 50 to 200 times a day without the EMG or help from the practitioner.

Incontinence is one of the most common conditions treated with biofeedback. In many cases, biofeedback treatment for incontinence is even covered by health insurance providers. (See Chapter 6 for more information on other physical conditions treated with biofeedback.)

HOW BIOFEEDBACK WORKS

How does biofeedback work? The University of Maryland Medical Center (UMMC) puts it simply: "Scientists are not able to explain exactly how or why biofeedback works." The UMMC does point out that biofeedback often works on conditions that are made worse by stress—relaxation, is the key to successful biofeedback treatment.[8]

Even though many respected organizations recognize biofeedback as effective, the treatment is not yet fully understood or proven. This lack of conclusive scientific evidence means biofeedback is considered an "alternative" form of medicine.

"Alternative" medicine can be used in addition to or instead of more traditional medical treatments, such as prescription medication. Doctors can usually explain how and why a medication works in the body, and they can prove its effects. Biofeedback, like many other alternative therapies, cannot be fully explained or proven by science. Because of its classification as an alternative treatment, not many people are aware of biofeedback treatment options. Unlike prescription medications, biofeedback is not advertised on mainstream television or in magazines or newspapers. As a result, many people only

Association of Applied Psychophysiology and Biofeedback

The Association of Applied Psychophysiology and Biofeedback (AAPB) is a nonprofit organization, started in 1969, that works to spread the knowledge and use of biofeedback. The AAPB provides regular courses, meetings, and publications on biofeedback and related topics and is well respected in the field.

Four times per year, the AAPB publishes the *AAPB Journal*, devoted to the study of applied psychophysiology and biofeedback. This is the only publication that concentrates on the science of this field. The organization also publishes *Biofeedback* magazine four times per year. To learn more about the AAPB, visit them online at http://www.aapb.org.

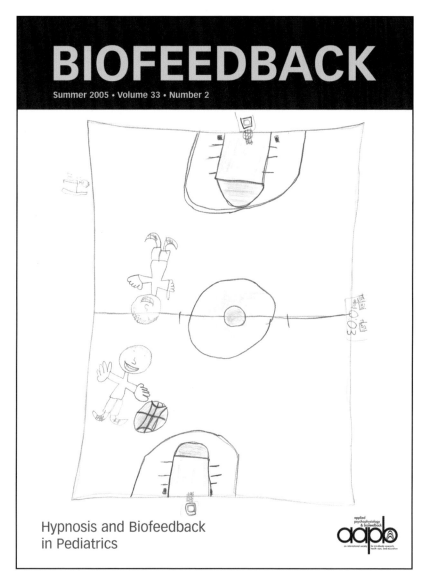

BIOFEEDBACK

Summer 2005 • Volume 33 • Number 2

Hypnosis and Biofeedback
in Pediatrics

Figure 2.4 The cover of this summer 2005 issue of *Biofeedback* magazine is a six-year-old child's drawing of a basketball game. As part of his biofeedback exercise, he imagines his favorite basketball team winning a game. When his team wins, he "wins" by decreasing his headache pain.

become aware of biofeedback treatment as an option if their doctor, a friend, or family member recommends it.

WHO USES BIOFEEDBACK?

Biofeedback can be used to treat patients with a wide variety of conditions. In general, patients turn to biofeedback treatment as a last resort when other more traditional methods fail. Many times the more traditional treatments involve prescription medication and counseling. For example, a patient suffering from depression may receive **antidepressant** medication first. If the first type of medication fails, he or she may try a different one, and then perhaps some counseling. If none of these traditional treatments alleviate the condition, the patient may try biofeedback.

Few hospitals or universities offer certified biofeedback treatment centers, but many large states, including California and New York, are home to private practice biofeedback clinics. In very specific situations, health insurance may cover biofeedback treatment, but in most cases, insurance does not cover it. Patients seeking biofeedback have some work to do to find and cover costs of treatment.

There are a handful of well-known and well-respected organizations and universities that support, teach, and practice biofeedback in the United States. All qualified biofeedback practitioners in the country are certified through the Biofeedback Certification Institute of America (BCIA).

Currently, BCIA has three certification programs: general, EEG, and Pelvic Muscle Dysfunction Biofeedback (PMDB). All candidates are required to hold a degree from a regionally accredited academic institution in a related field such as psychology, nursing, or physical therapy. Certification requirements include the completion of coursework, mentor program participation, a human anatomy/physiology course, and the successful completion of a written certification exam. To work independently when treating a medical or psychological diagnosis, BCIA requires their practitioners to carry a current, valid license/credential issued by the state in which they practice. Unlicensed providers must work under appropriate supervision when working with a medical or psychological diagnosis. Certification at both levels is valid for four years, three years for PMDB, after which time practitioners must prove that they have continued their education and have not been investigated for license violations.

The BCIA started certifying practitioners in 1981. According to Judy Crawford, the director of certification for the BCIA, about 100 people are certified each year. "We are stunned that it's not more," says Crawford. "But it's going to get more popular as insurance companies demand certification."[9]

HISTORY AND FUTURE OF BIOFEEDBACK

Biofeedback has been around for more than 50 years. Experts suggest that the field began to take shape in the United States in the 1950s with related health sciences such as physiology, psychology, and instrumentation engineering.

American Neal E. Miller (1909–2002) is often credited with first suggesting that people could train and control certain signals in the body just as they control movements of the body. Miller, an experimental psychologist at Yale University, came to his conclusions by mapping the brains of rats. He designed an experiment in which rats were rewarded when they successfully changed their heartbeat or blood pressure. With some training, the rats learned to control their brains and use them to alter heartbeat or blood pressure in order to get a reward. Such evidence suggested that the rats' brains could control bodily functions that are largely considered automatic. Miller suggested humans could do the same.

At the time, such an idea of controlling one's brain was quite radical. But by 1965, the first formal course in biofeedback was taught at Harvard University. Seven years later, the first major book on the topic, *The Handbook of Psychophysiology*, was published. Many professional publications about biofeedback followed. Between 1987 and 1991, about 150 publications on biofeedback were published each year.[10] According to Mark S. Schwartz and R. Paul Olson, writing in their book *Biofeedback: A Practitioner's Guide*, the number of publications is one measure of the history, growth, and future of a field. They suggest that, with hundreds of publications currently coming out every year, the field will continue to grow.

Still, much remains to be learned about biofeedback. Scientists are currently working to prove how current biofeedback treatments work (such as how a person controls his own brain waves). At the same time, biofeedback practitioners continue to pursue new ideas. In the words of Schwartz and Olson:

> This field [biofeedback] continues to attract advocates of bold and novel ideas. It allows the expression and cultivation of these ideas. It also allows criticism in the spirit of scientific debate. Biofeedback researchers and practitioners do not seek to dampen open inquiry and boldness. Had they done so, we would not have the many advances in knowledge and successful applications. . . .[11]

Because of this forward-looking approach, serious biofeedback researchers are not hampered by the lack of scientific explanation thus far. Many are working to explore new applications of biofeedback treatments to help skin conditions (ulcers and **herpes**), menopausal **hot flashes**, **insomnia**, and perhaps even **cancer.**

■ **Learn more about the contents of this chapter** Search the Internet for *applied psychophysiology, Biofeedback Certification Institute of America,* and *alternative medicine.*

3 | Brain Basics

Scientists use the words *mind* and *brain* to mean different things. The *mind* is the brain plus human consciousness, or thought. The *brain* alone is a very specific part of the body. The brain is a collection of 100 billion nerve cells and many other support cells that acts as the control center for the entire body.

Although scientists do not yet understand all the complex interactions that happen inside the brain, they have identified the basic pieces that make it work and how it controls and communicates with the body's different parts. This chapter gives a brief primer on brain basics so that biofeedback treatment can be better understood.

THE NERVOUS SYSTEM

The **nervous system** includes the brain, the spinal cord, and a complex network of cells that link all the pieces together (Figure 3.1). Through the nervous system, the brain regulates and controls how different parts of the body communicate with each other. Scientists divide the nervous system into two parts: the **central nervous system** and the **peripheral nervous system**.

The central nervous system includes the brain and the spinal cord. The brain is like a computer, where most of the

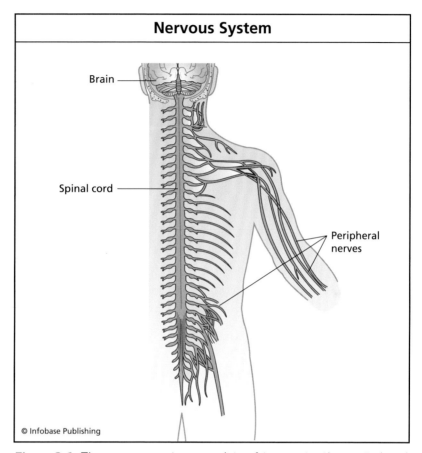

Nervous System

Brain

Spinal cord

Peripheral nerves

© Infobase Publishing

Figure 3.1 The nervous system consists of two parts: the central and peripheral nervous systems. The central nervous system consists of the brain and the spinal cord. The peripheral nervous system consists of nerves that relay information between the central nervous system and the distant parts of the body.

decision making and processing takes place; and the spinal cord is like a smart Internet cable, connecting the machine to a much larger network of parts and processing information gathered by those parts. The spinal cord begins at the base of the brain and physically connects the brain with the rest of the body. The job of the central nervous system is to process and move information.

The peripheral nervous system is the network of nerve cells outside of the brain and spinal cord that carry information to and from different parts of the body. This network of nerve cells is similar to an inbox full of e-mails—each e-mail contains a bit of information for the user to read, interpret, and take action. The job of the peripheral nervous system is to relay information to and from the brain and spinal cord to all the parts of the body.

THE NEURON

The workhorses of the nervous system are nerve cells, also called **neurons** (Figure 3.2). Scientists estimate that the brain contains about 100 billion neurons—a number so large that if you counted one neuron per second, it would take more than 3,000 years to count all the neurons in your brain.[12] Neurons carry messages throughout the body and are specifically designed for different jobs in the body. Neurons in the brain, for example, may have a different shape, size, and function than neurons in the skin, but all neurons have the same basic parts.

All neurons have two ends. One end, made up of branches known as dendrites, receives information. The other end, known as the axon, sends information out. Neurons use electrical signals and chemical signals to communicate. Electrical communication occurs within the neuron. All neurons use electrical signals to transmit information down their axon toward the dendrites of an adjacent neuron. These signals are the information often displayed as brain waves. When the electrical signal reaches the end of an axon, it releases a chemical signal. Chemical signals are molecules that contain information to tell the body how to react. Neurons transfer, or communicate, chemical signals to the dendrites in other neurons. Depending on the type of chemical signal, the receiving neuron may respond by creating a new electrical signal that races down its axon toward the next neuron in the chain.

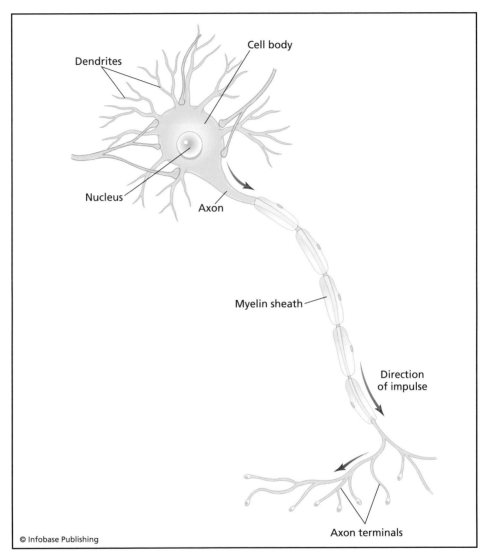

Figure 3.2 A neuron, also known as a nerve cell, transmits chemical and electrical signals throughout the body.

NEURON WIRING

Neurons connect to other neurons at **synapses** to create networks of nerve cells that can transmit information from place to place (Figure 3.3). Many synapses are formed in the womb before a baby is born, but these connections continue to develop as a person grows. The teen brain, for example, experiences a period of synapse formation in puberty. During this time, new synapses are formed and old synapses are destroyed, often in regions of the brain that are involved in planning, judgment, creativity, and emotion. Scientists believe that the brain adapts to form new synapses where they are needed and gets rid of synapses that are not being used.

There is also evidence that the adult brain can form new synapses when needed. In one experiment supporting this idea, researchers cut a nerve on the middle finger of an owl monkey, a mammal common in Central America and South America, rendering the finger immobile. Two months later, the researchers studied the brain of that monkey. Under normal conditions, the brain devotes equal space to control each finger in the hand. After the nerve was cut, the monkey's brain rewired itself. The areas of the brain that usually controlled the second and fourth fingers took over the area that had controlled the middle finger. These synapses for the middle finger were not being used, so the adult brain rewired itself to make those synapses more useful.

REWIRING THE BRAIN

From the brain's perspective, biofeedback is a two-step process. First, the brain must learn what the body is doing. The brain learns this information with the help of instruments, such as a thermometer, which can help make the body's signals available to the mind. Second, the brain has to find a way to control the signals.

If the brain is able to form new synapses during certain periods in a person's life, then perhaps such rewiring is part of the mechanism that makes biofeedback treatment effective against some conditions. Can a person consciously rewire his or her brain to fight off migraine headaches? To acquire control over a

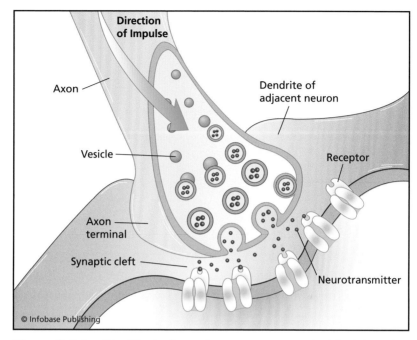

Figure 3.3 In this illustration of a synapse, an electrical impulse causes the release of neurotransmitters from vesicles at the end of a neuron. The neurotransmitters move across the synaptic cleft and attach to receptors on an adjacent neuron.

paralyzed limb? To slow down and relax the heart? The answers to such questions are not entirely clear. In fact, few scientists have even begun to explore these questions. But they are possibilities worth contemplating when learning about the brain and biofeedback. With some help, and a little practice, we may be able to tap into and harness more brain power than we think.

■ **Learn more about the contents of this chapter** Search the Internet for *nervous system*, *neuron*, and *neural development*.

4 | The Instruments

Biofeedback instruments help the mind read signals in the body and are a key part of the treatment process. According to an instruction manual for practitioners titled *Biofeedback: A Practitioner's Guide*, the instruments used in biofeedback have three tasks: (1) to monitor a signal from the body, (2) to measure what is monitored, and (3) to display what is monitored as meaningful information.

The signal can be temperature, brain waves, or some other body function. The instrument's job is to measure that signal and display it for the practitioner and patient. When the mind sees the measurement, it can make sense of what the body is doing.

Without the instrument readings, the mind does not always know exactly what the body is doing. Recall the skin temperature example. Can you tell the exact temperature of your skin without a thermometer? The thermometer is the instrument that makes the information of the temperature signal available to the mind. Some biofeedback instruments are quite simple; others are much more technical. The type of instrument used depends on the type of signal the mind is learning to read and the condition being treated. This chapter describes some of the instruments commonly used in biofeedback and how they work.

EVERYDAY OBJECTS AS INSTRUMENTS

In some cases, the instruments used in biofeedback are everyday objects. Books and mirrors, for example, can be used as instruments to indicate if a person is breathing from the correct place in the body. Breathing from the **abdomen**, the space between the chest and the hips, is a helpful relaxation skill. Biofeedback practitioners often teach this type of breathing to help people slow down the body and focus the mind. It is not difficult to do, but it can be hard to know if you are doing it correctly. In this case, abdominal breathing is the signal, and very simple instruments can help the mind read that signal correctly.

One simple instrument used by practitioners is a book—hardcover or paperback, large or small. It doesn't matter which book is used as long as the patient and practitioner can see it. To use the book as a biofeedback instrument, a patient lies flat on his back and places a book on his abdomen. When the patient breathes from his chest, the book will not move. When the patient breathes from his abdomen, the book will clearly rise and fall. The patient's mind sees the book rise and fall and recognizes when breathing is performed correctly. The book has become an instrument.

A mirror works in a similar way. When a patient breathes correctly from his abdomen, he will be able to see his stomach rise and fall by looking at his profile in a mirror. The mind sees movement in the mirror and the signal of the movement confirms that breathing is being done correctly.

Even another person can be used as an instrument in the same breathing exercise. One person places her hand on the abdomen of another person and can feel the abdomen rise and fall. By telling the breather what she feels, the first person makes the information available and the breather knows if he is breathing correctly. Such everyday objects (and people) used as instruments are most helpful in breathing exercises.

TEMPERATURE AND CIRCULATORY SYSTEM MONITORS

A thermometer is a simple instrument that measures temperature. Biofeedback practitioners often use heat-sensitive probes that are taped on the skin (Figure 4.1). The probes detect heat from the skin and the temperature information is transmitted through wires to a monitor.

Less precise thermometers are often used in home biofeedback treatments without the help of a practitioner. Thin paper-strip thermometers are laid on the skin. The strips contain a crystal liquid that changes color when heated. Bulb thermometers

Biofeedback in Action: Lie Detectors

Sometimes the body speaks louder than the mind—or at least speaks more truthfully than the mind. For nearly a century, experts have used signals in the body to determine whether a person is telling the truth.

Lie detectors, or polygraphs, measure three signals in the body: breathing, sweat, and heart rate. The person connected to the polygraph answers questions while signals in the body are being recorded. The signals are then displayed either on paper or on a computer monitor. Once the questions are completed, an expert will examine the polygraph's record of the signals to determine whether the person is telling the truth. The method is controversial, but it is used regularly by federal, state, and local law enforcement agencies in the United States. Each state decides whether polygraph tests can be used as evidence in court.

To learn more about polygraphs, visit the Web site of the American Polygraph Association at www.polygraph.org.

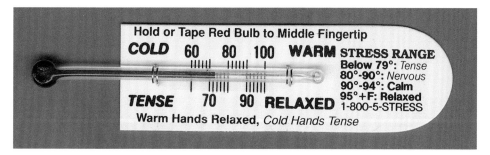

Figure 4.1 A glass tube thermometer is a tool used by practitioners of biofeedback. The thermometer is taped to a person's finger, not only revealing the temperature of the skin but also indicating the movement of blood in the body. The movement of blood reveals how relaxed a person is feeling, which then indicates whether the relaxation exercises are working.

contain a heat-sensitive liquid that expands when it gets warm and climbs up a temperature chart. These thermometers do work, but they are not as reliable as the probes. In addition, old bulb thermometers contain mercury, a poisonous liquid metal, that is dangerous if it leaks.

To use a thermometer as a biofeedback instrument, the practitioner first tapes the thermometer probe on the skin—usually on the side of a finger. When the patient reads the temperature on the monitor, his mind learns the skin temperature of his body. The thermometer has become an instrument to translate a body signal for the mind. The skin temperature itself is not really important, but it tells the practitioner how blood is moving in the body. How blood is moving in the body is an indication of how relaxed a person feels.

Blood moves through the body in thin, pipe-like tubes called blood **vessels**. When a person is relaxed, the vessels relax and open wide. This allows more blood to flow, warming the body first and the hands and feet last. Warm skin temperatures on the hands mean a person is very relaxed. When a person is tense, the vessels tighten and constrict. This reduces blood flow in the body. Because the hands and feet are the farthest from the heart (the place from where blood is pumped), they get cold first. Cold hands and feet can be a sign of stress or anxiety.

Because skin temperature changes fairly quickly, practitioners use it as a measure of relaxation. A patient may begin a treatment session tense, with cold hands. As a practitioner works on relaxing the patient with visual imagery, breathing, and counseling, the skin temperature of the hands should get warmer. The thermometer tells the patient and the practitioner if the relaxation exercises are working.

Another sign of relaxation is a person's level of vasoconstriction, which is a measure of how narrow, or constricted, the blood vessels are. A **finger phototransmitter** is a small sensor that clips softly to a patient's fingertip and uses light to measure vasoconstriction. The finger phototransmitter shines a small light through the finger's blood vessels. The light is then reflected back to the sensor. The amount of light reflected tells the practitioner what the blood vessels are doing. Narrow blood vessels hold less blood, and less blood allows more light to be reflected. Relaxed, open vessels hold more blood, and more blood blocks more light. The more the light is blocked, the more blood is flowing in the vessels.

The measure of heart rate patterns over time is called **heart rate variability** (HRV). Monitors for HRV work by measuring the time between each heartbeat and determining the change in the time between each beat. In healthy people, the exact HRV is always changing—sometimes beating fast, sometimes slow, with no clear pattern. In less healthy people, the HRV is very steady and doesn't change easily. Many studies show that people who have had heart attacks or high blood pressure have an unchanging HRV.

In biofeedback, patients learn to change their HRV. Fear, excitement, or exercise will increase the HRV, while slow breathing and relaxation will decrease it. In HRV biofeedback, it is the ability to change the HRV that is important. A patient and practitioner sit together and watch the heart rate activity. With coaching, imagery, and relaxation exercises, the practitioner helps the patient learn to control the beats of his or her heart. Although the mechanisms by which HRV training works are unknown, it has been used as an effective treatment for lung problems such as **asthma.**

SWEAT AND MUSCLE TENSION

Galvanic skin response (GSR) monitors indicate how much a person is sweating by measuring how much electricity can pass through the skin (Figure 4.2). Some GSR monitors produce a tiny current of electricity and are connected to the fingertips or palm of the hand, where many sweat glands are present. These monitors measure the skin's ability to resist passing an electrical current.

More sweat produces more salt, which means more electricity the skin can conduct. Sweat, like skin temperature, can be an indicator of how relaxed or tense a person feels. More sweat indicates anxiety or stress; less sweat indicates relaxation. Like skin temperature, the amount of sweat changes fairly quickly, and practitioners use it as a measure of relaxation. As a practitioner and patient work through relaxation techniques, the GSR monitor lets them know if the exercises are working.

Like sweat, muscle tension can be a sign of stress or anxiety. An electromyograph (EMG) is an instrument that records the electrical signals produced when a muscle gets tense, or contracts (Figure 4.3). Muscles produce electricity when they contract. When more muscles contract, more electricity is produced. In biofeedback, small EMG sensors are placed on the surface of the skin to detect the amount of electricity being produced by the muscles. Practitioners call this surface

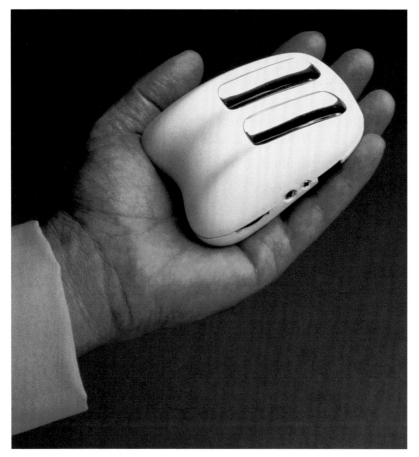

Figure 4.2 A galvanic skin response (GSR) device monitors the amount of electricity passing through the skin. The GSR device measures the skin's ability to resist the small amounts of electric current produced by the GSR device, thus indicating a person's level of stress.

EMG, or SEMG for short. SEMG is used to find places in the body where the muscles are tenser than they need to be. The shoulder muscles, for example, often get tense when a person is under stress. Habitual stress causing shoulder muscle tension becomes a problem when the muscles do not relax once the stressful situation is resolved. Muscles that stay tense for

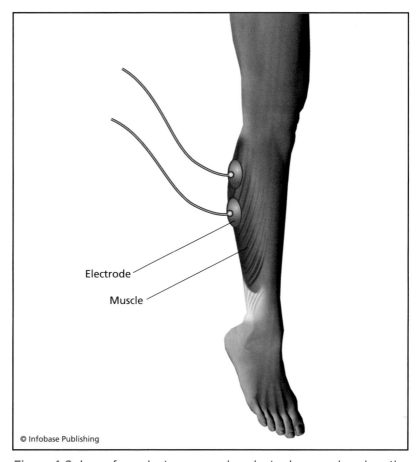

Figure 4.3 In surface electromyography, electrodes are placed on the skin to measure the amount of electricity produced when a muscle contracts. Biofeedback uses surface electromyography to help a patient learn to relax his or her muscles.

too long can hurt. People with long-term muscle pain, who become so accustomed to muscle tension, sometimes can not tell which muscles are tense and which are not. The SEMG can help them pinpoint which muscles need to be relaxed, and the biofeedback practitioner can help the patient learn to relax those muscles.

The SEMG monitor tells the practitioner and patient immediately whether the exercises are working. SEMG biofeedback is used to treat a wide variety of conditions including tension headaches, incontinence, muscle spasms, and paralysis.

College Students Measure Sweat

At the University of Texas at Austin Counseling and Mental Health Center (CMHC), college students are using galvanic skin response instruments to practice biofeedback relaxation techniques on their own.

The Mind/Body Lab at the CMHC is equipped with leather recliners and touch-screen computers that guide students through self-controlled relaxation exercises. Users check out a galvanic skin response instrument, receive a five-minute lesson on how it works, and monitor their own bodies as they complete each self-guided relaxation exercise. As students learn to relax, they can watch the galvanic skin response monitor. High measurements indicate high stress levels. Low measurements indicate low stress levels, which show students that the relaxation exercises are working.

"The instruments are very simple," says Assistant Director Chris Brownson, who designed the lab so that resident students could make easy, free, and unscheduled appointments. "We wanted to create an environment for students where they could explore the relationship between the mind and body," said Brownson. "The goal is to help students deal with the high levels of stress often associated with college."[*]

The Mind/Body Lab has been quite popular since it opened in February 2005, according to Brownson and his coworkers. Other universities are planning to open similar facilities for students, but all are still in the planning stages.

* Chris Brownson, personal communication with author, June 23, 2006.

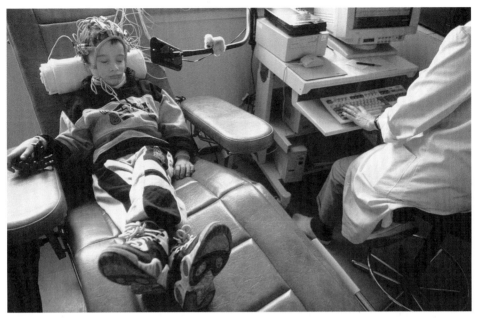

Figure 4.4 A young boy undergoes an electroencephalogram, which is a test that measures the electrical activity of the brain. Electrodes on his scalp detect brain waves, which are then displayed on a monitor.

BRAIN WAVE INSTRUMENTS

An electroencephalograph (EEG) is an instrument that measures the electrical activity of the brain and displays it as waves on a monitor (Figure 4.4). A practitioner places small, metal sensors on the scalp of a patient. The practitioner will place the sensors to target the brain waves of interest for that patient; different brain waves are displayed, depending on where the sensors are placed.

To really understand how EEGs work, it helps to understand a bit more about the brain waves they measure. Brain waves are the electrical signals produced by neurons in the brain. Like waves in the ocean, brain waves come in different shapes and sizes. Waves can be large, small, slow, fast, uniform, or variable. Different parts of the brain produce different brain waves depending on what each part of the brain is doing at any moment.

BRAIN WAVE	RECORDING LOCATION IN BRAIN	ROLE IN BODY
Alpha	Back (can be recorded in other places)	Associated with physical calmness and lack of activity.
Beta	Front and center	Seen when the mind is alert or actively dreaming.
Gamma	Everywhere	Observed when the brain responds to specific things (like clicking noises or flashing lights) or does a specific, complex task.
Theta	Back	Constantly present when awake (some suggest there are two different types of theta waves).
Delta	Everywhere	Seen in deep sleep and comas.

* Note that almost all parts of the brain can produce each type of wave. "Head location" refers to one common place on the head where biofeedback practitioners often record this type of wave.

There are five main types of brain waves used in biofeedback (Figure 4.5), but there are many other brain waves not described here. The main types of brain waves are each named after a letter of the Greek alphabet: alpha, beta, gamma, theta, and delta waves. Each type of wave has its own shape and size.

In brain wave biofeedback, or neurofeedback, the EEG is used to help patients learn to change their brain wave patterns. In this case, the brain waves are the signals and the EEG allows the patient and practitioner to see the brain wave patterns on a monitor. By sitting together with the patient, the practitioner can use different strategies to help the patient change the brain wave patterns of interest. The patient may be asked to focus on a task and increase levels of concentration or to relax the mind using positive imagery. The patient can see how his or her thoughts influence the brain wave pattern displayed

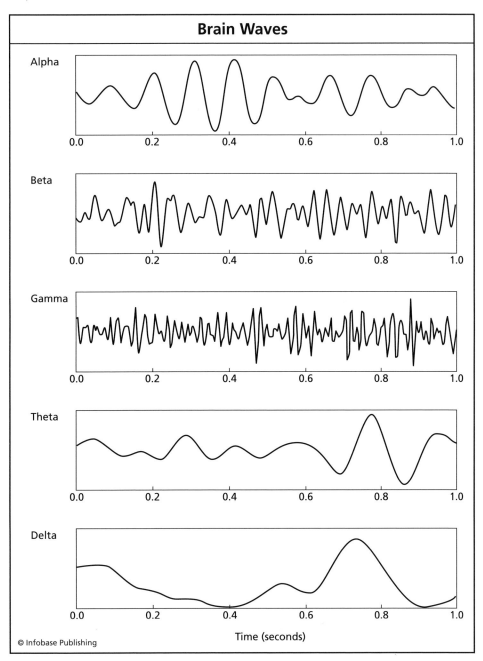

Figure 4.5 The five main types of brain waves used in biofeedback each have a characteristic shape and size. Practitioners read the characteristic wave signals in a patient's brain and use that information to treat mind and body conditions.

on the monitor, and might be "rewarded" for changing the wave patterns. Children, for example, often play computer games with their minds during biofeedback treatments. The games only run when the child produces the correct pattern of brain waves.

Over time, the patient learns to change the brain waves on demand, without help from the EEG monitor. This technique is used to treat many different mind and body conditions, including behavioral disorders, **ADHD**, epilepsy, **substance addiction**, and more.

■ **Learn more about the contents of this chapter** Search the Internet for *finger photo transmitter*, *galvanic skin response*, and *electroencephalograph.*

Biofeedback and Mental Conditions

Biofeedback is used to treat many different mental conditions. Mental conditions affect mood and behavior and include anxiety disorders, depression, and attention deficit disorder. This chapter defines some mental conditions that are treated with biofeedback, describes how they are treated, and explores some current scientific research on these conditions.

STRESS

Stress is a physical or behavioral condition that causes tension in the mind and body. Everyone, every day, experiences some level of stress. Small, short-lived amounts of stress can motivate you to do things, such as get out of bed and go to school. Large levels of long-duration stress can have harmful effects on your body, such as heart trouble and muscle aches. Relaxation is the opposite of stress and is often described as a "loose" and "comfortable" feeling.

It is difficult to estimate the number of people who suffer from severe amounts of stress. According to the National Institute of Mental Health, about 40 million Americans over 18 years of age have an anxiety disorder, and nearly three-quarters of those with an anxiety disorder will have their first episode of an anxiety attack before the age of 21.[13]

Severe anxiety disorders are often accompanied by depression. Treating these conditions depends heavily on the particular patient. In some cases, biofeedback relaxation treatments are used to combat high levels of stress.

Biofeedback Treatment of Stress

In biofeedback, the definition of stress is more strictly defined. Using biofeedback instruments (including thermometers, heart rate monitors, and galvanic skin response monitors), practitioners can define stress and relaxation with physical measurements of signals in the body. For example, one of the simplest forms of biofeedback relaxation uses skin temperature measurements to determine the impact of positive thinking and imagery. A practitioner and patient sit together and a thermometer measures the skin temperature of the patient's hands. The practitioner coaches the patient to think about positive, relaxing thoughts and may show various images to him or her. The images can be of peaceful places and people or other happy thoughts. The coaching depends entirely on the practitioner—there are no specific requirements.

Skin temperature becomes a measure of how relaxed the patient feels during these exercises. Instead of relying on a verbal response such as "I feel relaxed now," the patient can read his skin temperature to see whether his body is responding to the relaxation coaching. Warm skin temperature indicates a relaxed body.

Relaxation biofeedback is often used together with other forms of biofeedback treatment. A practitioner might begin with simple relaxation exercises and move on to more complicated treatments.

Spotlight on Research: Treating Stressed-out Kids

As a mother of five, long-time university professor, and biofeedback practitioner, Dr. Elizabeth Stroebel knows a little something about kids and stress. Stroebel specializes in helping young people learn to recognize stress in the body, so that they can manage levels of stress over time. Stroebel spends a lot of time talking with kids who are stressed out. She might start with a simple question such as, "What's hurting your heart today?" In her work, the answers might include migraine headaches, movement disorders (such as repeated kicking and hair pulling), respiratory diseases, and cancer side effects.

Once the source of the stress is established, Stroebel helps kids recognize and control it using biofeedback. One six-year-old, for example, quickly learned to identify a person with a headache based on visibly tense muscles in the forehead. "Kids are so observant," Stroebel says. "They just need to learn what to look for."[14] Stroebel has created a self-guided stress management program for children and families, called the Kiddie Quieting Reflex (or Kiddie QR for short), that uses audio CDs and colorful characters. In the future, she hopes to develop an affordable, portable biofeedback treatment box that children can take with them wherever they go.

DEPRESSION

With depression, the lines between different mind-related conditions begin to blur. Depression rarely occurs by itself; it is often accompanied by anxiety disorders and headaches. Treating such a mix of conditions can be difficult. Traditional treatment of severe depression includes antidepressant medication, a drug that affects how chemical substances act in the brain. Most experts agree that severe depression needs to be treated with antidepressant medication before any type of biofeedback treatment begins.

Biofeedback Treatment of Depression

To treat depression with brain wave biofeedback, practitioners concentrate on three types of brain waves: alpha, theta, and beta. Practitioners target these waves because people with depression have different levels of alpha and theta waves.

Biofeedback training teaches patients to inhibit or enhance these waves as needed.

At the same time, beta wave training can help strengthen the brain for recovery. Experts sometimes call this the "kindling effect." It occurs when a painful memory resides in the brain for so long that it changes from a mental injury to something resembling a physical injury. The mental injury can be treated with therapy, but the symptoms from the physical injury—including a short attention span and bad memory—are more difficult to treat. Training beta waves is one treatment option, but again, there is little scientific evidence to support this idea.

Like many biofeedback treatments, brain wave biofeedback treatment of depression works for some patients and not others. Researchers cannot explain why. For example, one practitioner counseled a woman with depression for one hour a week for seven years with little progress. After one course of brain wave biofeedback, the woman improved "miraculously." The same practitioner treated a second depression patient with the same brain wave biofeedback and failed to see any improvement at all.[15]

Spotlight on Research: Altering Pain Perception

Dr. J. Peter Rosenfeld, a professor in the psychology department at Northwestern University in Evanston, Illinois, is an expert on brain waves. In the 1980s, he discovered that brain wave biofeedback could be used to alter pain perception in mice. Rosenfeld taught mice to increase their pain threshold (the point at which pain becomes noticeable) by altering their brain wave patterns. The mice were rewarded for successfully doing so, and soon they became conditioned to resist pain.

Rosenfeld soon decided to apply similar techniques to people suffering from depression. First he had to figure out which brain waves to target to treat depression, which involved finding out which brain waves are associated with our positive and negative emotions—not an easy task. Building on research from other scientists, Rosenfeld's research group suggested that depressed people have low levels of brain wave activity in the front-left part of the brain. The researchers successfully trained 9 out of 13 people to increase these brain waves but did not relate the increase to a change in emotion.

Although there is some evidence that depression can be alleviated with changes to these specific brain waves, scientific studies to confirm this theory have not been performed. To do so would require depressed and non-depressed patients in controlled settings over long periods of time—a situation that is difficult to create. Today, Rosenfeld continues his work with brain waves, but his attention is focused on how brain wave patterns change when a person is telling a lie.[16]

ATTENTION DEFICIT HYPERACTIVITY DISORDER

Attention Deficit Hyperactivity Disorder (ADHD) affects a person's ability to concentrate and is one of the most common mental disorders among children. Symptoms include hyperactivity, forgetfulness, moodiness, and distractibility. ADHD, and the closely related Attention Deficit Disorder (ADD), are considered chronic, or long-term, disorders with no real cures. The National Institute of Mental Health (NIMH) estimates that between 3% and 5% of children in the United States—about 2 million kids—have ADHD.[17] That means that in a classroom of 25 to 30 students, at least one will have the disorder.

Traditional treatment of ADHD includes medication (Figure 5.1). There are many different types of medications used to treat it, but all of them are considered stimulants. A **stimulant** is a drug that increases activity in a particular part of the nervous system and makes a user feel more awake and alert. The NIMH reports that about 1 in 10 children with ADHD is not helped by

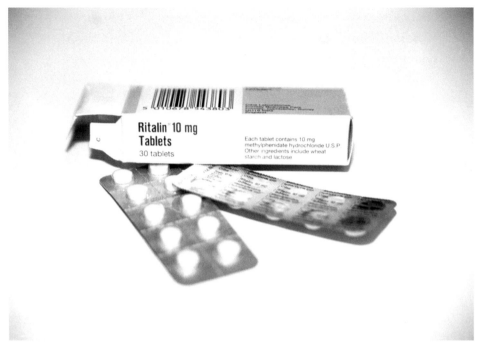

Figure 5.1 Ritalin pills *(above)* are used to treat patients diagnosed with attention deficit disorder (ADD). It contains the drug methylphenidate, which is a central nervous system stimulant. Biofeedback is used as an alternative method of treatment of ADD, especially in patients who do not respond well to Ritalin.

stimulant medication.[18] For these children, biofeedback targeting brain wave signals may be an alternative form of treatment.

Biofeedback Treatment of ADHD

Researchers have learned that people with ADHD or ADD have slower theta brain waves in the front-central parts of the brain. To help a patient adjust these wave patterns, a practitioner first connects the patient up to an EEG so that brain waves can be displayed on a monitor. Next, the practitioner determines which waves need to change to affect behavior. In general, patients learn to produce beta waves when they need to concentrate and alpha waves when they need to relax, all without creating more slow-moving theta waves. The practitioner will sit with the patient as they both watch the brain wave monitor. The patient will be guided verbally to change the brain wave patterns. Some patients learn to change waves by thinking specific thoughts. Other people learn by focusing on a task, such as a video game.

In the video game treatment, the patient plays the game not with a traditional joystick or hand controls but with his mind. By changing certain brain wave patterns, a patient moves a character in the game. As the patient learns to control his brain waves, he gets to play the game. Eventually, the patient learns to change brain wave patterns on demand, without guidance from the practitioner or the game. Such changes can result in children who are better able to concentrate in school and focus on tasks.

When asked, patients do not know how they produce different brain waves or why they begin to act differently. Some scientists say the important thing is not how patients change brain waves, but that they know how to do it on demand. Other scientists are skeptical that the treatment works at all. Regardless, experts estimate that there are more than 1,200 organizations in the United States, Australia, Israel, Europe, and Japan using brain wave biofeedback as a treatment for ADHD.[19] In many cases, brain wave biofeedback is used along with medication to treat ADHD.

Spotlight on Research: Treating ADHD

In the 1970s, researcher Dr. Joel F. Lubar was one of the first people to use brain wave biofeedback to treat patients with ADHD. Initially, his research involved helping patients with epilepsy and seizures alter their brain waves to improve their ability to pay attention and focus. When this method worked, Lubar suggested trying a similar approach with children suffering from ADHD. Dr. Lubar soon discovered that brain wave patterns of children with ADHD were different from those of children without the condition. Lubar and his colleagues were able to teach children to improve their behavior by increasing their amounts of fast-moving brain waves.

During the past 30 years, there has been more research on the relationship between ADHD and brain wave patterns. According to Lubar, "ADHD treatment with brain wave biofeedback has become the most widely-used [treatment] in the field."[20] Although not everyone would agree that these treatments are effective, there is a huge demand for training in this field.

Today, Lubar codirects the Southeastern Biofeedback Institute (SBI) in Knoxville, Tennessee, an organization that trains practitioners, studies treatments, and provides brain wave biofeedback. The SBI is one of the few organizations that provides training for certification in brain wave biofeedback from the Biofeedback Certification Institute of America.

PERFORMANCE ANXIETY

Scientists know that performance artists, including musicians and actors, often suffer from psychiatric disorders. This is not to say that all performers are sick, but that performers, as a group, have high rates of mood, anxiety, eating, and sleeping disorders.[21]

Anxiety, in particular, can affect performance artists in a negative way. Anxiety is a combination of negative emotions including fear and worry that can cause cold, sweaty hands, racing heartbeats, breathlessness, and muscle tension. Too much anxiety affects a person's performance ability. A musician with sore, tense hands, for example, may have a hard time playing a piece of music the way he or she wants to. By treating performance anxiety with biofeedback, practitioners hope to rid performers of the physical conditions that affect their work.

Biofeedback Treatment of Performance Anxiety

In one case, biofeedback practitioners treated a pianist's anxiety using muscle movements as the signal. The practitioner connected the patient's forearms to an EMG and displayed the muscle tension levels on a monitor. The patient learned that every time she felt uncertain about a piece of music, the muscle tension in her forearms increased. The practitioner helped the woman relieve her muscle tension by practicing ways to learn a piece of music more thoroughly and to alleviate her uncertainty. Over time, the woman learned to control her levels of anxiety (and therefore her muscle tension) on her own. She began to perform more often and without pain.[22]

EMG biofeedback is perhaps the most common type of biofeedback used to treat performance anxiety, but other biofeedback methods are also used. Relaxation and skin temperature training is used to help performers control stress levels, and EEG biofeedback is used to help performers increase their ability to concentrate. The type of biofeedback treatment depends on the particulars of the patient. Experts suggest that a practitioner must first learn the patient's type of muscle pain, performance history, and general mental health before beginning treatment.

Spotlight on Research: Improving Performance Art

Neuroscientist Dr. Tobias Egner, now a research fellow at Columbia University in New York, studies how people use their brains to focus and pay attention. Early in his career, Egner and his colleagues explored the importance of focusing in performing musicians. Egner's research group taught music students in London how to increase their ability to focus by creating more beta waves in their brains. At the same time, the young musicians learned to create alpha and theta waves to help them relax.

The researchers discovered that the overall musical performance ratings (as determined by independent experts) went up after brain wave biofeedback training. The musicians made fewer errors, and ratings of "stylistic accuracy," "emotional commitment and conviction," and "interpretive imagination" were strong.[23] "Self-regulation through means of biofeedback holds promising potential for enhancing musical performance," wrote Egner.[24] As is the case with many forms of biofeedback treatment, no one knows exactly why or how this works. The next step for researchers will more closely monitor what happens in the brain of performers.

SUBSTANCE ADDICTION

Substance addiction is the repeated use of something, such as cigarettes or alcohol, until a person becomes dependent on that substance. Because there are many different levels of addiction and many substances to be addicted to, estimating the number of people suffering from these conditions is nearly impossible. The National Institute on Drug Abuse supports much of the scientific research in this field and works to make the information available to lawmakers, health care providers, and the public.

Biofeedback Treatment of Substance Addiction

Biofeedback treatment of substance addiction is often a combination of relaxation biofeedback and brain wave biofeedback. Patients begin with relaxation biofeedback treatments and slowly move into brain wave biofeedback sessions.

The goal of this treatment is to teach the patient to increase alpha and theta brain waves. In a typical session, the patient relaxes in a comfortable chair while watching his EEG with the practitioner who guides the patient to imagine rejecting the drug, becoming clean and sober, and becoming the person he wants to be. With repeated sessions (sometimes as many as 30), the patient begins to respond in the ways he imagined. Often, experts say, the addiction simply goes away. Through visualization of positive images, the patient learns to alter his or her brain waves during treatment sessions. Compared to other bio-feedback treatments for mental conditions, use of biofeedback to treat substance addiction is a relatively new area of research. Again, no one really understands why or how it works, but researchers continue to learn more.

Spotlight on Research: Helping Alcoholics

Psychologist Dr. Eugene Peniston was one of the first scientists to publish experimental results using brain wave biofeedback to treat patients with substance addiction. In the 1980s, Peniston compared treatment results for 30 men. Ten were alcoholics who received alpha and theta biofeedback training in addition to traditional, talk therapy treatment; 10 were alcoholics who received only traditional, talk therapy treatment; and 10 were not alcoholics who did not receive any treatments, but completed all the same tests and measurements as the other two groups.

After one month of near-daily treatments, 8 of the 10 alcoholics receiving brain wave biofeedback training had stopped drinking, and only one of them returned to drinking within three years. All 10 of the men receiving only talk therapy returned to their addictions almost immediately when the therapy session ended.

This study marked the first time brain wave biofeedback was shown to help treat substance addiction. Today, Peniston is a researcher at the Sam Rayburn Memorial Veterans' Center in Bonham, Texas.[25]

■ **Learn more about the contents of this chapter** Search the Internet for *anxiety disorders*, *attention deficit disorder*, and *National Institute of Mental Health*.

6 Biofeedback and Physical Conditions

Biofeedback is also used to treat many physical conditions. Physical conditions affect muscles and movement and include headaches, asthma, and paralysis. This chapter defines some physical conditions that are sometimes treated with biofeedback, describes how they are treated, and explores current research exploring these conditions.

HEADACHES

In general, a headache is simply pain that is felt in the head. A tension headache is a particular type of headache that is often caused by muscle pain in the head, neck, and back. Muscles that stay tense over time often cause these pains. Tension headaches are one of the most common forms of pain in adults and children. One study showed that 56% of boys and 74% of girls between the ages of 12 and 17 years get at least one headache every four weeks.[26] Most people take an over-the-counter painkiller such as ibuprofen or aspirin to treat headache pain. Biofeedback is another treatment option.

Biofeedback Treatment of Headaches

Biofeedback practitioners often begin treatment by trying to determine and eliminate the cause of the headache.

Eliminating a particular food, changing a sitting position, or altering some other daily habit can make some tension headaches go away. If the first treatment method is unsuccessful, EMG and relaxation biofeedback methods can be used to treat headaches.

There is some evidence that simple relaxation and stress management exercises (see Chapter 5) help eliminate headaches. Biofeedback relaxation treatments work to change physiological processes in the body (such as increasing blood flow), with the hopes of alleviating headache pain. A summary of headache research shows that this treatment is effective in treating 59% of tension headaches.[27]

EMG biofeedback is also used to treat tension headaches. A practitioner attaches sensors to the head, neck, or shoulders of the patient (depending on where the pain is located). Next, the practitioner and patient watch the EMG monitor and actively try to lower muscle tension. This treatment targets specific muscles or areas of the body where pain occurs. Research shows that this method effectively treats 61% of tension headaches.[28]

In the past 30 years, experts estimate biofeedback has been used to treat hundreds of thousands of people with tension headaches.[29] Scientists still cannot explain exactly why or how biofeedback treatment works to reduce headache pain. Does more blood flow to the head alleviate pain, remove stress, and relax the muscles? The mechanisms that make this work are unclear. This lack of a scientific explanation makes biofeedback treatment for headaches somewhat vulnerable to criticism. According to the health insurance provider Blue Cross Blue Shield, "evidence is insufficient to demonstrate the effectiveness of biofeedback for treatment of tension or migraine headaches."[30] Other people, including many who have spent careers studying the effects of biofeedback treatment on headaches, strongly disagree.

Spotlight on Research: Treating Kids with Headaches

Dr. Frank Andrasik started studying biofeedback treatment for headaches as a graduate student working toward a doctoral degree in the mid-1970s. Early in his research, he decided to focus his work on children with headaches, for two reasons. First, he believed children who got headaches needed treatment, and second, if he could rid children of headaches, then they would not grow up to be adults with headaches.

One of Andrasik's early studies examined the effectiveness of skin temperature biofeedback to relieve children of headache pain. Nine children, ages 10 to 14 years old, received 10 one-hour-long biofeedback relaxation treatment sessions. They were also instructed to practice the same skills alone and with a parent at home. The children kept a daily diary of headache pain during and after the treatments.

At the end of the study, 7 of the 9 children improved the frequency and intensity of their headaches. The other 2 children improved their headaches, but not by much. The study gave support to the use of temperature biofeedback treatment of headaches, and Andrasik was able to continue his work with similar studies and larger groups of children.

ASTHMA

Asthma is a long-term disease that causes irritated, obstructed airways in the lungs (Figure 6.1). People with asthma may have a hard time exercising and breathing when it's cold outside, and they may wheeze often. According to the National Heart, Lung, and Blood Institute, asthma is one of the most common long-term conditions in the United States. About 15 million people have asthma and 1.5 million people visit the emergency room for asthma treatment each year.[31]

Asthma can be made worse by certain activities, infections, or environmental factors such as dust. Asthma can also be affected

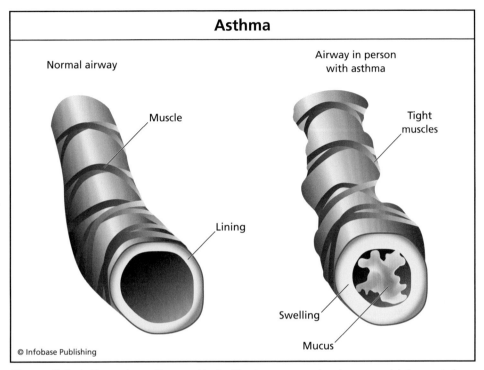

Asthma

Normal airway

Airway in person
with asthma

Muscle

Tight
muscles

Lining

Swelling

Mucus

© Infobase Publishing

Figure 6.1 Asthma is a disease that affects a person's airways, which are tubes carrying air in and out of the lungs. People who suffer from asthma have inflamed airways with an excessive amount of mucus. The image above is a side-by-side view of a person with healthy airways *(left)* and a person who suffers from asthma *(right)*.

by anxiety, stress, and sadness. Asthma caused by these events can often be treated successfully with biofeedback.

Biofeedback Treatment of Asthma

To treat asthma with biofeedback, practitioners concentrate on a patient's anxiety and stress levels. A practitioner might begin with basic abdominal breathing and relaxation exercises to treat the mind and then use EMG biofeedback to treat the body. A practitioner connects the EMG sensors to the patient's neck and throat muscles and then works to reduce muscle tension in those areas. Some studies have shown that EMG biofeedback treatment for asthma improves a patient's ability to breathe, but heart rate biofeedback treatment may have a stronger impact on asthma patients.

A practitioner monitors the heart rate variability of an asthma patient and coaches her to change the rhythm of her heartbeats. Some evidence suggests that the effects of asthma decrease when patients learn to increase their HRV while slowing their breathing. This may be the result of slow, deep breathing, which is known to protect against asthma. As is the case with many forms of biofeedback, no one is quite sure why or how this treatment works. Study results of biofeedback's effect on asthma are promising but mixed.

Spotlight on Research: Attacking Asthma

Dr. Paul Lehrer has always been interested in the ability to self-regulate, or control certain things in the body. He was the first person to test the effects of many self-regulation exercises on asthma, including stress management, yoga, and HRV biofeedback. Lehrer's research began almost by accident when he decided to learn more about how the respiratory system regulates itself in the body. At about the same time, he discovered he had a mild case of asthma and began working with other scientists studying the impact of behavior on the body.

Lehrer tried using relaxation biofeedback to treat asthma, but it did not work very well. Next he experimented with HRV biofeedback. Lehrer treated asthma patients with HRV biofeedback for 10 weeks. After this training, patients learned to increase their HRV and showed significant improvements in asthma symptoms.[32] It was the first time asthma was successfully treated with biofeedback.

Today, Lehrer is the director of the Center for Stress Management and Behavioral Medicine and a professor of psychiatry at the Robert Wood Johnson Medical School in Piscataway, New Jersey. He continues to study how people can control the symptoms of asthma, epilepsy, and other conditions.

INCONTINENCE

Incontinence is the involuntary excretion of urine through the urethra or solid waste through the anus. A person who is incontinent cannot control the muscles that allow for these excretions. The condition is not uncommon.

Biofeedback Treatment of Incontinence

To treat incontinence with biofeedback, practitioners use two different types of EMGs to monitor muscle tension. EMG sensors can be inserted into the vagina, or birth canal, of women to detect muscle tension in the bladder. In men, the sensor is inserted into the urethra in the penis. EMG sensors can also be inserted into the anus, where rectal muscle tension is detected.

After sensors are inserted, the practitioner measures the resting levels of the muscles. The patient is then asked to contract his muscles as if he were trying to stop the flow of urine or a bowel movement and to hold the contraction for 10 seconds. The practitioner records the level of muscle tension observed during this time. The same procedure may be repeated several times. The practitioner may then use a different set of EMG sensors, perhaps on the surface of the skin surrounding the abdomen, to measure different muscles. During this procedure, the patient receives a record of muscle tension and works with the practitioner to alter the EMG response as needed.

Positive imagery and reinforcement are also used to help the patient learn to control these muscles. At the same time, patients might be asked to exercise these muscles and strengthen their ability to control the flow of waste products from the body. Exercises known as Kegels are commonly prescribed to women who have just given birth. In some cases, giving birth weakens the muscles that control the excretion of urine. Kegel exercises strengthen those muscles.

Of all the different applications of biofeedback, treatment of incontinence with biofeedback is widely recognized as effective. In many circumstances, biofeedback incontinence treatment is recommended by doctors and covered by insurance companies.

Spotlight on Research: Exercising to Treat Incontinence

More than 50 years ago, a gynecologist named Dr. Arnold Kegel developed the exercises designed to strengthen the muscles that

False Feedback

False feedback is the process of giving biofeedback patients incorrect information to see how their minds respond. In one example, researchers gave headache patients undergoing biofeedback treatment false verbal praise and indications of success. That is, they made the patients think the treatments were working well. Later, these patients reported reductions in headache symptoms. The mind believed that the treatment worked, and the patients reported feeling less physical pain. Such research supports the idea that the mind controls the way the body feels in some way, but scientists do not yet understand all the details.

In part, this helps explain why biofeedback treatments might work on some patients and not others. Some people suggest whether a treatment works depends on the way a patient thinks about the body. Whatever the reason for pain reduction, scientists agree that false feedback should never be used as a serious approach to therapy. It is only used in controlled experiments to learn more about the mind-body connection.

control wastes passing out of the body. Initially, he developed the exercises as a way for women to control incontinence after childbirth. He soon realized the exercises worked for anyone experiencing incontinence.

To perform a Kegel, patients flex the muscles on the floor of the pelvis, which are the muscles that stop the flow of urine. To be sure the procedure is done correctly, many sources suggest sitting on the toilet and beginning to urinate, and then stopping the flow of urine midstream. When the flow of urine stops, patients know that their muscles are moving correctly. Once a person identifies which muscles should be targeted, the exercises can be done outside of the bathroom. The exercise is repeated and muscle contractions should be held for 10 seconds each time.[33]

EPILEPSY

Epilepsy is a brain disorder in which clusters of nerve cells generate unusual electrical signals. People with epilepsy may experience strange sensations and emotions, muscle convulsions, and loss of consciousness. Such disruptions in brain activity can lead to seizures.

Epilepsy is one of the most common neurological disorders. For every 1,000 people, there are 5 to 10 people with epilepsy. The condition is most likely to occur either during the first 10 years or after the age of 60.[34] There is no cure for epilepsy, but seizures in about 80% of its sufferers can be controlled with medication or surgery.[35] More recently, biofeedback has also become an option to treat epilepsy.

Biofeedback Treatment of Epilepsy

To treat epilepsy with biofeedback, practitioners use EEG instruments to monitor brain wave patterns. During these treatment sessions, practitioners watch for the **slow cortical potential** (SCP). The SCP is a positive or negative change in certain types of brain waves. SCPs are different from other brain waves in that they are larger and easier for most patients to control or produce on demand.

People with epilepsy also often use a **thought translation device**, a computer controlled by a person's SCP waves (Figure 6.2). The patient sits in a comfortable chair with EEG sensors—connected to a thought translation device—on his head. The patient looks at a computer screen, which has a small cursor that rises when the patient moves his SCPs in a negatively charged direction. When the SCPs move in a positive direction, the cursor drops downward. The challenge is to learn to move the cursor up or down on demand. By focusing on certain thoughts, such as sinking a basketball or winning a reward, patients learn how to move the cursor on the screen.

In each treatment session, the patient moves the cursor hundreds of times. In some versions, the movement becomes a soccer game. When the patient moves the "ball" through the correct "goal," he scores a point and sees a smiling face on the screen. After multiple treatment sessions with the thought translation device, the patient learns to move the cursor in the correct direction 70% to 80% of the time.[36]

This new skill can then be used to help control seizures. Levels of SCPs increase, either positively or negatively, before a seizure. The hope is that patients learn to recognize this change in brain waves and consciously bring it under control before the seizure occurs.

Spotlight on Research: Settling Seizures

Sleep researcher Dr. M. Barry Sterman first discovered that the ability to control one's own brain waves might help guard against seizures. But he didn't begin by researching people. It all started with sleeping cats.

Sterman was tracking the EEGs of cats as part of another research project in the late 1960s when he realized that certain

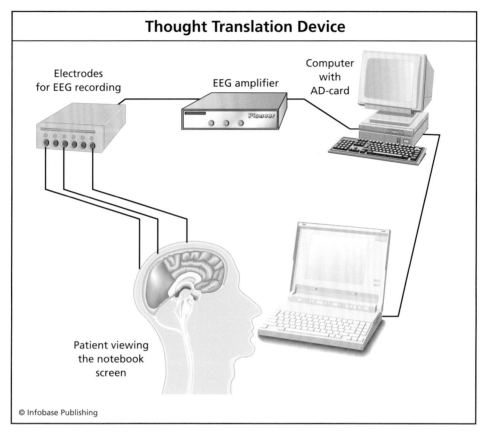

Thought Translation Device

Electrodes for EEG recording

EEG amplifier

Computer with AD-card

Patient viewing the notebook screen

© Infobase Publishing

Figure 6.2 The brain waves of a patient are measured and amplified, then fed into a special computer that translates these brain waves into actions on a computer screen. Using this method, a patient can move a cursor on a computer screen and ultimately communicate using only brain waves.

brain waves got stronger when the cats received snacks. These experiments eventually showed that the cats could change their brain waves at will.

As part of another experiment, Sterman injected the cats with a chemical known to induce seizures. Most of the cats suffered seizures within an hour. But the cats that had been trained to strengthen their brain waves in the snack experiments did not experience seizures until much later, and some didn't experience seizures at all.[37] Sterman soon explored how similar brain wave training could help people guard against seizures.

Scientists continue this work today. Sterman is currently professor emeritus in the departments of neurobiology and biobehavioral psychiatry at the University of California at Los Angeles.

PARALYSIS

Paralysis is the complete loss of muscle movement at one or more locations in the body. People who are completely paralyzed may not be able to move any part of the body. This type of paralysis is often caused by damage to the brain and/or spinal cord.

Estimating the number of paralyzed people in the United States is difficult because no government agency maintains these statistics. One source based in Australia estimates that about 2.4 million people in the United States (just less than 1%) suffer from some form of paralysis.[38]

Biofeedback Treatment of Paralysis

Biofeedback practitioners have targeted one form of paralysis known as locked-in syndrome. People with this condition are able to think, hear, feel, and learn—but they cannot move any part of the body. In some of these cases, biofeedback practitioners have tried using the thought translation device.

During the first session with the device, EEG sensors are attached to the head of the paralyzed person so that his own brain waves control the computer screen. The patient is asked to "play" with the computer cursor by thinking different types of thoughts. Sad thoughts might make the cursor move in one direction. Happy thoughts might make it move in another direction. This playtime is intended to let the patient become more familiar with the device.

In the next session, the patient learns to control the SCP brain waves that move the cursor on the computer screen. When the cursor moves in the correct direction, the patient sees a smiley face on the screen. The practitioner does not tell the patient what to think, because there is no clear way to change one's brain waves. The patient figures it out by watching the cursor on the screen.

Once a patient masters moving the cursor, she begins to match symbols. A row of symbols at the bottom of the screen appears. A symbol is presented to the patient, who then selects the same symbol on the screen. In this stage, incorrect selections are ignored so the patient is not "punished" for making a mistake. At the next level, patients begin to copy spelling. A word appears on the screen and the patient types the same word by selecting letters with the cursor. When a wrong letter is selected, the computer lets the patient know of the mistake by returning to the previous level of difficulty. Words start short and get longer as the patient improves.

The final step allows the patient to spell words freely. In this step, the paralyzed patient can communicate whatever he wants by typing the words on the screen using his own brain waves. In this case, biofeedback treatment teaches the patient to control SCP brain waves, and then lets him use those brain waves to communicate.

Spotlight on Research: Communicating with a Computer

German neuroscientist Dr. Niels Birbaumer invented the thought translation device in the mid-1990s to give people with paralysis and nerve disorders a way to communicate. The device was one of the first creations in a category of instruments now known as brain-computer interfaces (BCIs). BCIs allow paralyzed people to communicate with the world.

Using BCIs, patients learn to move a cursor on a computer screen using SCP brain waves and eventually learn to select letters from the bottom of a screen to type out words (Figure 6.3). The process is slow and it can take up to an hour to pick 100 letters,[39] but it provides a way for paralyzed people to "talk."

Figure 6.3 German scientist Dr. Niels Birbaumer invented a device that provides people with paralysis and nerve disorders the ability to communicate. Dr. Birbaumer's invention, the thought translation device, allows for patients to move cursors on a computer screen using brain waves, as demonstrated in the above photo.

From early in his career, Birbaumer studied SCPs—brain waves that occur over a period of seconds. He has studied these and other brain waves in musicians, people who are blind, people with epilepsy, and paralyzed patients. Birbaumer is a professor at the University of Tübingen in Germany.

■ **Learn more about the contents of this chapter** Search the Internet for *National Heart, Lung, and Blood Institute*; *Kegel exercises*; and *brain-computer interfaces*.

7 | Biofeedback and You

Biofeedback treatment can have multiple benefits. It can help a person reduce or eliminate medication, treat conditions that have not responded to medications, and better understand and monitor his or her own body. At the same time, biofeedback treatments are not completely understood and some people are hesitant to pursue such methods without really knowing what happens in the body. If you are considering biofeedback treatment for yourself, you should weigh the benefits and disadvantages of biofeedback for your specific situation. If you decide to pursue biofeedback treatment for a condition you have, there are a few steps you can take to get started.

STEP 1: RELAX

To get a feel for biofeedback and how it works, start with simple relaxation or stress management biofeedback treatments. These are arguably the simplest, most widely used types of biofeedback, and they provide a good place to get some introductory, hands-on experience.

If you want to explore the idea more fully, find out if there are any informal biofeedback opportunities where you live. If you are lucky, you may be near a place where you can use unscheduled, self-guided biofeedback tools (see Chapter 4 sidebar on the University of Texas).

Biofeedback Games

There are a few different biofeedback-based "games" on the market that help children and adults practice relaxation and abdominal breathing techniques at home. These games often use simple biofeedback instruments to determine whether the exercises are helping the users relax.

Master-Quest: Pathways to Inward Journeys is a computer-based game on CD, designed to teach children to relax using deep breathing. Children first learn to recognize stress in their bodies and then practice abdominal

A demonstration of The Journey to Wild Divine.

breathing and muscle relaxation. In this case, users measure their skin temperature with a strip thermometer to determine whether the breathing exercises are helping them relax.

The Journey to Wild Divine is another computer-based game that also teaches relaxation and deep breathing. Like *Master Quest*, this game uses mythical "guides" and soft, spiritual language to describe what's happening. But underneath the figurative language are real, physical measurements. In Wild Divine, users track the body's heart rate variability (HRV) to determine whether the breathing exercises are working. When a player successfully controls his HRV, he "wins" that level of the game and advances to the next round.

STEP 2: RESEARCH

Once you've gotten a taste for biofeedback by practicing relaxation and stress management exercises, start thinking more about your specific condition. Although there is evidence that biofeedback treatment helps with about 150 different medical conditions,[40] the effectiveness of biofeedback has been studied on some conditions more than others. Well-studied conditions include stress, depression, ADHD, headaches, and incontinence. If you have another condition, do some research. Find out if your symptoms can be treated with biofeedback and if anyone has studied its effectiveness.

Next, ask your doctor if he or she thinks biofeedback is right for you. Although biofeedback is widely considered safe, there are some conditions that are more sensitive to biofeedback than others. Experts at the Mayo Clinic recommend talking to your doctor before you try biofeedback if you have depression, severe psychosis, or diabetes. In some cases, biofeedback can interfere with diabetes medications (including insulin).[41]

STEP 3: COVER COSTS

Many experts say biofeedback got a bad name in the 1960s because it became associated with certain hippie cultures that used the term loosely to describe a range of unscientific "treatments." Biofeedback was considered "alternative" in a negative way. Today, despite legitimate scientific research performed and published on the effectiveness of biofeedback treatment, it is still considered "alternative" or "complementary" to more traditional medical treatments. In fact, science has not explained many of the mechanisms of biofeedback. How, for example, does thinking about shooting a basketball change a person's SCP levels? No one really knows. Because biofeedback cannot be explained and has not been thoroughly researched with large, **controlled studies**, health insurance providers do not usually recognize it as a viable treatment option; therefore, insurance companies will not cover the costs.

Incontinence is one insurance success story. Medicare, the federally funded health insurance program for seniors, specifically covers the cost of biofeedback incontinence treatment when more traditional muscle exercises do not work.[42] Prior to this federal decision in the year 2000, whether biofeedback treatment costs for incontinence were covered depended on the judgment of individual health insurance providers—some covered it and some did not.

Many insurance companies cover biofeedback treatment costs for a very specific list of conditions. Such coverage depends on where you live, your condition, and your health insurance provider. You can ask your doctor if treatment is covered, but the best way to find out if you have coverage is to contact your health insurance provider.

STEP 4: FIND AN EXPERT

If you decide to pursue biofeedback treatment, finding the right certified biofeedback practitioner is perhaps the most important step you can take. You need to look for two things: a Biofeedback Certification Institute of America (BCIA)–certified practitioner, and a biofeedback expert who is knowledgeable about your condition. At the moment, there are no laws governing who can perform biofeedback treatment. Anyone can call himself a "practitioner," purchase some instruments, and open a biofeedback treatment center. This, in part, is why insurance companies do not always cover biofeedback. Only consider biofeedback practitioners who are certified by the BCIA. This assures that you are treated by a professional who has had some coursework, training, and testing, and who has kept those credentials current.

It also helps to find a biofeedback practitioner with experience treating your specific condition. There are many different kinds of biofeedback—such as HRV biofeedback, EMG bio-feedback, and EEG biofeedback. You would not go to a dentist to treat a broken foot, for example, so you shouldn't go to an HRV biofeedback practitioner to treat a muscle tension head-ache. Because of the nature of biofeedback, it is not always clear which treatment option is best for a specific condition. Biofeedback seeks to make the mind more aware of signals in the body to strengthen the mind-body connection. In theory, any biofeedback practitioner could treat any condition if he or she has the instruments. You should seek out a biofeedback expert on your condition because that person will simply have more experience treating patients with similar ailments. The practi-tioner will know the instruments and how to use them and will

Biofeedback Certification Institute of America

The Biofeedback Certification Institute of America (BCIA) was formed in 1981 to "establish and maintain professional stan-dards for the provision of biofeedback services and to certify those who meet these standards."[*] It is the only certification organization in the United States, and the only certification organization recognized worldwide.

The BCIA is a nonprofit organization of biofeedback practitio-ners, researchers, and educators. The BCIA works to maintain professional standards and services in biofeedback. The orga-nization offers three main types of certification: general, EEG, and Pelvic Muscle Dysfunction Biofeedback (PMDB). Many practitioners maintain certification in multiple areas of biofeed-back. To learn more about the BCIA, visit them online at www. bcia.org.

[*] Biofeedback Certification Institute of America, http://www.bcia. org (accessed November 30, 2006).

have experience looking at those specific signals displayed by the body. It's not that an EEG-based treatment could never help a muscle-related condition, but a muscle expert might have more knowledge about how to handle a muscle-related condition.

STEP 5: GO

Once you have researched your condition and the costs of treatment, and have located a certified practitioner, it's time to give biofeedback a try. When you go for your first session, expect to be there 30 to 60 minutes unless you are told otherwise in

Figure 7.1 Journaling is an important part of biofeedback treatment. It is highly recommended by biofeedback practitioners that the patient document his or her symptoms, feelings, and experiences throughout the process. Keeping a journal helps the patient keep track of the effectiveness of biofeedback.

advance. During this time, you will likely get sensors stuck to your skin that connect you to some type of instrument. As you know, the instrument will read the signals in your body and display them on a monitor for you and the practitioner to see.

In many cases, the first session will simply help educate you and the practitioner about your specific condition. It is unlikely that you will be miraculously cured by the end of your first visit. Don't be too surprised or discouraged if the session unfolds differently than you expected. Each practitioner is different.

To track the progress of your biofeedback treatments, experts at the Mayo Clinic suggest keeping a detailed, written history of your experience.[43] Describe in a notebook how you feel before, during, and after the treatment (Figure 7.1). Keep daily notes about your symptoms and when you use the treatment outside of formal sessions. Over time, this will help you keep track of your condition and the effectiveness of the treatment sessions. Many practitioners may ask you to keep such a diary. If they don't, start one anyway.

■ **Learn more about the contents of this chapter** Search the Internet for *home biofeedback*, *biofeedback health insurance*, and *biofeedback games*.

8 | The Future of Biofeedback

Ask almost any devoted practitioner about the future of biofeedback, and he or she will be quick to say that biofeedback is a health care revolution waiting to happen. The treatment gives the body the power to heal itself without the use of drugs or surgeries. But to actually replace—or even be considered equal to—traditional medicine, biofeedback has some major roadblocks to overcome. This chapter lists the three major challenges biofeedback faces.

THE REPUTATION CHALLENGE

Biofeedback still suffers from its 1960s reputation as a far-out alternative form of medicine. The National Institutes of Health (NIH) and the Centers for Disease Control and Prevention (CDC) are two large, well-respected federal organizations that describe biofeedback as "alternative."

The NIH relegates biofeedback to one of its divisions called the National Center for Complementary and Alternative Medicine. Here, biofeedback is described alongside "energy medicine," magnet therapy, green tea, and garlic.[44] The CDC describes biofeedback as a "mind-body therapy" along with hypnosis and yoga.[45] Though some of these alternative forms of medicine may indeed be effective, most biofeedback practitioners and researchers are quick to disagree with placing biofeedback in the "alternative" category. Biofeedback, they say, is supported by real science that has simply not yet been recognized by the general population.

Biofeedback's alternative reputation is so strong and so undesirable, even some leading biofeedback researchers avoid the term altogether. Niels Birbaumer, for example, the creator of the thought translation device that lets paralyzed people communicate using brain waves, prefers to call his work "physiological regulation."[46] He deliberately avoids associating his work with the alternative reputation of biofeedback.

Biofeedback Defined

Some leading biofeedback researchers avoid the word *biofeedback* altogether. It is difficult to define and is plagued by an "alternative" reputation. *Neurofeedback* and *applied psychophysiology* are often more desirable and have more specific definitions.

Biofeedback	A process that teaches the mind to read and respond to signals in the body, such as skin temperature, brain waves, and muscle movements.
Neurofeedback	A process that teaches the mind to control brain wave activity. A type of biofeedback.
Applied psychophysiology	A more technical term that encompasses evaluation, diagnosis, education, treatment, and performance enhancement. Scientific researchers prefer this term, but have yet to agree on an exact definition.

Even the leading professional organization appears to be avoiding the word *biofeedback*. The Biofeedback Research Society has long been a leader in the field but recently changed its name to the Association for Applied Psychophysiology and Biofeedback, perhaps to deemphasize the term *biofeedback*.

THE SCIENCE CHALLENGE

The science supporting biofeedback is constantly taking shape. Most people agree that more controlled studies are needed to "prove" that biofeedback works and how. A controlled study uses two (or more) groups of subjects who are studied in identical conditions except for the treatment being tested. For example, suppose 20 children receive biofeedback relaxation treatment for anxiety and that after two weeks all 20 children suffer stress-related breakdowns. In this situation, it is difficult to determine what caused the breakdowns. Did the treatment fail terribly? Did a public tragedy occur that affected all the children equally? The cause is unknown.

To avoid this problem, a controlled study might assign half the children to a biofeedback relaxation treatment group and the other half of the children to a group that does not receive biofeedback treatment. In this experiment, the stress response of the two groups can be compared. If a public tragedy did occur, and the children who received biofeedback relaxation treatments were able to deal with the events while the untreated group suffered stress-related breakdowns, then this experiment would provide evidence that the treatment was effective in some way.

There are some controlled studies published on the effectiveness of biofeedback treatments, most notably for asthma, incontinence, and ADHD, but such studies are difficult to get funded. To perform this type of study, as with all scientific research, researchers first have to find an organization willing to pay for the work. Organizations do not have much motivation to fund controlled scientific studies of biofeedback treatments because there isn't much money to be made. There won't be any new drugs or equipment to sell, so there is not much motivation to do the research other than to learn more about the treatment process.[47]

Even when controlled biofeedback studies are funded, they tend to be small, involving fairly small numbers of participants. The size of the study makes it difficult for scientists to draw broad conclusions. If the biofeedback relaxation treatment really did prove effective on the 20 research subjects, does that mean the same method will work on the entire population of children in the country? Scientists can use statistics to help calculate how the general population will respond to a treatment, but they are careful to make such statements.

The Association for Applied Psychophysiology and Biofeedback is careful as well. For example, AAPB officially says that brain wave biofeedback treatments are "probably efficacious." That is, the treatments probably work. Tom Collura, president of the AAPB Neurofeedback Division, explains, "we are very careful about our own work; perhaps more reserved than needed."[48]

THE INSURANCE CHALLENGE

The AAPB is constantly working to convince insurance companies to cover the costs of biofeedback treatments. In some cases, the federal government determines whether a specific treatment is covered. In other cases it is left up to each state to decide.

Incontinence, for example, was approved by the federal government for coverage in 2000. This means all insurance companies are required to cover biofeedback treatment of this condition when ordered by a doctor; it is not up for debate. Headaches are different. There is no federal law that says

University Programs

More and more universities are offering formal degrees in biofeedback. As the next generation of university students chooses career paths, such programs could be in high demand. The Biofeedback Certification Institute of America recognizes biofeedback coursework at these universities:

UNIVERSITY	
Northern Arizona University Flagstaff, Arizona	http://www4.nau.edu/hpc/faq.htm
Sonoma State University Novato, California	http://www.sonoma.edu/ psychology/biofeedback/
Nova Southeastern University Ft. Lauderdale, Florida	http://www.nova.edu/biofeedback/
Boise State University Boise, Idaho	http://www.boisestate.edu
Kansas State University Manhattan, Kansas	http://www.k-state.edu/counseling/ training/bfcert.htm
University of Maryland-Baltimore Baltimore, Maryland	http://nursing.umaryland.edu/ faculty/fch/kverno.htm
Truman State University Kirksville, Missouri	http://www.truman.edu
East Carolina University Greenville, North Carolina	http://www.ecu.edu/rcls/ biofeedback/
University of North Texas Denton, Texas	http://www.coe.unt.edu/cdhe/ Biofeedback1.htm
St. Mary's University San Antonio, Texas	http://www.stmarytx.edu

insurance companies must cover the cost of biofeedback treatment for headaches, so insurance providers decide whether to cover the cost of headache treatments on a case-by-case basis, even if that treatment has been ordered by a doctor. Coverage varies among states and among patients.

It is not entirely clear what is required of a treatment in order to be covered by health insurance companies. Some commonly covered treatments would not meet the scientific standards set out by the AAPB.[49] The organization is actively gathering information, performing research, and writing position papers to get health insurance coverage for specific biofeedback treatments. Such coverage, some say, would finally help biofeedback shake its "alternative" label and become a mainstream treatment option widely recognized by doctors and patients.

THE NEXT GENERATION

If the goal of biofeedback treatment is simply to unite the mind and the body, then the number of different conditions potentially helped with this method is nearly limitless. Although biofeedback is used regularly for only a handful of common conditions, its effectiveness on many other conditions is currently being researched. The instruction manual for biofeedback practitioners, *Biofeedback: A Practitioner's Guide*, lists well over a dozen new conditions that may be helped with biofeedback. In most of these conditions, only a few research studies have been performed and the results have been mixed. Yet experts suggest that these conditions—ones that are often unresponsive to traditional drug treatments—are promising new targets for the future of biofeedback. The rest of this chapter describes some of these conditions, beginning with the most researched, and summarizes what scientists have learned so far.

Figure 8.1 Insomnia, the inability to fall asleep, can often be treated with bio-feedback therapy and relaxation techniques. Insomnia is often caused by anxiety. Biofeedback monitors help target anxiety, hoping to change behavioral problems.

Insomnia

Insomnia is an inability to fall asleep that is often caused by an inexplicable inability to relax (Figure 8.1). Experts estimate between 9% and 12% of adults suffer from insomnia regularly.[50]

To treat insomnia with biofeedback, practitioners have used relaxation, EMG, and brain wave biofeedback for many decades. In this case, studies can't really be conducted in the home when a person is actually trying to fall asleep in his own bed. Instead, scientists recreate a sleeping situation during the daytime, usu-ally in an office setting. A typical treatment session might begin with relaxation and EMG biofeedback. The patient is asked to lie down while the practitioner monitors hand temperature and muscle tension in the front of the head. The researcher monitors these signals from the body before and after she asks the patient to relax as if he wanted to sleep.

In some cases, the suggestion of trying to sleep makes the patient anxious and less relaxed. The biofeedback monitors help the practitioner and the patient learn more about this anxiety so that they can target the most troublesome times. Some evidence suggests that patients who suffer from anxiety-related insomnia benefit from theta wave biofeedback treatment, but how this compares to other forms of treatment is still unknown.

Writer's Cramp

Writer's cramp occurs when a person starts to write and the muscles in the hand and wrist malfunction, causing excess gripping or releasing of the pen or pencil. Writer's cramp is a rare condition but is completely disabling and resistant to most traditional treatments including medication, massage therapy, and exercise.

To treat writer's cramp with biofeedback, practitioners use EMG instruments to better understand the muscle movements in the hand and wrist. The practitioner teaches patients what their muscles are doing and helps them learn to relax those muscles with the help of the instruments.

Scientists first began testing the effectiveness of EMG biofeedback on writer's cramp in the mid-1980s but had mixed results. These initial studies focused the EMG instruments on the muscles in the hand and wrist. Later studies used EMG biofeedback to monitor muscles not only in the hand and wrist, but also in the forearms. These treatments proved more effective.

In one study, researchers used EMG biofeedback to treat eight people with "tremor" type writer's cramp, in which the hand begins to shake uncontrollably when the person starts to write. After weekly treatment sessions, 25% (two patients) showed marked improvement, 25% showed moderate improvement, and 25% showed mild improvement. Although this study is small and the level of improvement is small, biofeedback treatment seems to be one of the most effective tools to fight writer's cramp.

Menopausal Hot Flashes

Hot flashes are short periods of extremely uncomfortable, heavy sweating, either at night or during the day, that occur during menopause. Menopause is a hormonal change women go through, often around age 50, after which they no longer menstruate and are not able to become pregnant. Most women experience hot flashes for at least one year during menopause, and some can have hot flashes for more than five years.[51]

To treat this condition with biofeedback, practitioners use relaxation biofeedback to teach women to breathe deeply and from the abdomen. Scientists have learned that women change the way they breathe prior to a hot flash. Women often take many short breaths and feel breathless even when they are resting quietly. The use of biofeedback breathing to treat hot flashes has been researched in a handful of controlled studies.

In one study, 11 women were taught to breathe more slowly and regularly over the course of eight treatment sessions. Instruments helped the women see when and how they were breathing. After these sessions, the number of hot flashes experienced by the patients dropped from about 15 per day to 10 per day.[52] Experts suggest refinements to these treatments could lead to even better results.

Biofeedback treatment of hot flashes could be an attractive option for women wishing to avoid hormone therapy. Traditionally, women take extra doses of the female hormone called estrogen to treat hot flashes, but the side effects of such therapy are not entirely desirable. Other treatments include changing one's diet, quitting smoking, and exercising.

Herpes

Herpes is viral disease that can cause painful blisters on the mouth, lips, or genitals. A person who has herpes carries the virus, the organism that causes the disease, all the time. The symptoms of the disease, in this case the painful blisters, only appear occasionally. Scientists know that the blisters are more likely to appear when a person feels stress.

To treat herpes with biofeedback, practitioners use stress-relaxation biofeedback treatments. The idea is to relax the patient, therefore easing the painful blisters of the herpes virus. There are few reports of the effectiveness of this treatment, but initial studies have been completed. In the 1990s, one researcher tested the effectiveness of relaxation biofeedback on eight people with herpes. Each person received just three treatment sessions, and five of them reported 40% to 93% reductions in blister outbreaks that lasted for at least three months.[53]

Treatment of herpes with biofeedback relaxation is uncommon and unproven but it is just one of the skin diseases that may be targeted by this method in the future. Other skin diseases include ulcers, psoriasis (red bumps on the skin), and eczema (dry skin).

Cancer

Cancer is a group of disorders in which the cells in the body multiply uncontrollably and invade other parts of the body. Such invaders can usually be controlled by the body's **immune system**, the complex network of cells designed to defend against such invasions. With cancer, the immune system does not work as well as it should, for unknown reasons.

To treat cancer with biofeedback, practitioners target the immune system. There is some evidence that stress and the brain influence the effectiveness of the body's immune system, so biofeedback's goal is to relax the mind and body in order to strengthen the body's defenses.

It is not entirely clear if and how this works. In one study, researchers used relaxation, guided imagery, and EMG biofeedback to influence the immune systems of 13 cancer patients. Researchers were able to increase the number of defensive cells

Will Telehealth Take Over?

Although it sounds like a science fiction story, the concept of telehealth is not that farfetched. Telehealth uses computers and information technology to educate and treat patients in the comfort of their own home or office. Instead of going to the doctor to be treated for a condition, a patient might log on to the Internet and follow a set of instructions to administer a self-treatment.

Biofeedback is a good candidate for such telehealth services and some researchers have already explored its use. In one case, a practitioner located in Hawaii used real-time audio and video to provide relaxation biofeedback treatment sessions for patients located in remote areas in Korea, Japan, and Guam.*

There are few reasons, in theory, why such tele-treatments should not work, but there are many challenges to making tele-treatment practical in everyday life. The cost of computer equipment and connections to the Internet, practitioner licenses and authenticity, consent for treatment, and other legal liability coverage concerns quickly complicate the idea of telehealth biofeedback. Nevertheless, in the modern age of cell phones, PDAs, and instant messaging, the convenience of communication is expected. The ability to communicate easily with a doctor or a biofeedback practitioner probably isn't that far in the future.

* Mark S. Schwartz, and Frank Andrasik, *Biofeedback: A Practitioner's Guide*. New York: Guilford Press, 2003, 901.

in the immune system within several weeks. This and other studies are enough to create some interest in biofeedback treatments for cancer, but experts agree that many challenges remain in this area and many more studies are required.

BIOFEEDBACK TOMORROW

The mechanisms that make biofeedback work are not fully understood. But look at biofeedback from a broader perspective and the current lack of scientific support is not that unusual. So much of science, throughout history, has happened by accident. Penicillin, for example, the widely used, bacteria-fighting drug, was first discovered when neglected, overgrown cultures of organisms were mixed together accidentally. The scientist in charge, a Scottish physician named Alexander Fleming, noticed an area around a culture where bacteria had not been able to grow like the others. Something had stopped the growth. Fleming isolated the organism from the clear area and identified it as a mold called penicillin. He studied the organism for the next 10 years and began testing it against diseases to see what would happen. Fleming did not know how it worked, but he soon realized that it killed certain types of infections in the body. It took another decade to develop the drug into a viable treatment for the public.

Penicillin was developed and put into use without a clear understanding of what was happening in the body. People used the drug because it worked, but the science to explain the mechanism came much later. Biofeedback, perhaps, is not that different. Only time will tell.

■ Learn more about the contents of this chapter Search the Internet for *psychophysiology degree*, *telehealth*, and *biofeedback coursework*.

Notes

1. Tim Robbins, *A Symphony in the Brain.* New York: Grove Press, 2000, 5–31.
2. Susan Antelis, e-mail message to author, July 23, 2006.
3. Robbins, 92–104.
4. Nicola Neumann, and Niels Birbaumer, "Thinking Out Loud," *Scientific American Mind.* New York: Scientific American, 2004, 78–83.
5. Susan Antelis, e-mail message to author, July 23, 2006.
6. Mental Health America, "Depression: What You Need to Know," http://www.nmha.org/index.cfm?objectid=C7DF94A1-1372-4D20-C81EDE3D3BB4474C (accessed December 6, 2006) and "Depression in Teens," http://www.nmha.org/index.cfm?objectid=C7DF950F-1372-4D20-C8B5BD8DFDD94CF1 (accessed December 6, 2006).
7. National Kidney and Urologic Diseases Information Clearinghouse, "Urinary Incontinence in Women," http://kidney.niddk.nih.gov/kudiseases/pubs/uiwomen/ (accessed December 6, 2006).
8. University of Maryland Medical Center, "Biofeedback," http://www.umm.edu/altmed/ConsModalities/Biofeedbackcm.html (accessed December 5, 2006).
9. Judy Crawford, personal communication with author, July 12, 2006.
10. Mark S. Schwartz and Frank Andrasik, *Biofeedback: A Practitioner's Guide.* New York: Guilford Press, 2003, 13.
11. Ibid., 909.
12. Jennifer R. Morgan and Ona Bloom. *Cells of the Nervous System.* New York: Chelsea House Publishers, 2006, 14.
13. National Institute of Mental Health, "The Numbers Count: Mental Disorders in Americans," http://www.nimh.nih.gov/publicat/numbers.cfm (accessed December 5, 2006).
14. Liz Stroebel, personal communication with author, July 15, 2006.
15. Robbins, 178–179.
16. J. Peter Rosenfeld, personal communication with author, July 5, 2006.
17. National Institute of Mental Health, National Institutes of Health, "Attention Deficit Hyperactivity Disorder," http://www.nimh.nih.gov/publicat/adhd.cfm (accessed December 5, 2006).
18. Ibid.
19. Schwartz and Andrasik, 409.
20. Joel F. Lubar, personal communication with author, July 7, 2006.
21. Schwartz and Andrasik, 545.
22. Frank Andrasik, "Relaxation and Biofeedback for Chronic Headaches," in *Pain Management* Sonora, Calif.: American Academy of Pain Management, 1986, 553–554.

23. J.H. Gruzelier, and T. Egner, "Physiological Self-regulation: Biofeedback and Neurofeedback," in *Musical Excellence: Strategies and Techniques to Enhance Performance*, ed. A. Williamson, 197–219 London: Oxford University Press, 2004.

24. Ibid.

25. Robbins, 158–164.

26. Schwartz and Andrasik, 687.

27. Andrasik, 213–239.

28. Ibid.

29. Schwartz and Andrasik, 275.

30. Blue Cross Blue Shield, "Medical Policy: Biofeedback as a Treatment of Headache," http://www.regence.com/trgmedpol/alliedHealth/ah27.html (accessed December 5, 2006).

31. National Heart, Lung, and Blood Institute, National Institutes of Health, "Data Fact Sheet: Asthma Statistics," 1999, http://www.nhlbi.nih.gov/health/prof/lung/asthma/asthstat.pdf (accessed December 5, 2006).

32. P. Lehrer, E. Vaschillo, S. Lu, et al., "Heart Rate Variability Biofeedback: Effects of Age on Heart Rate Variability, Baroreflex Gain, and Asthma," *Clinical Investigations*. 129, no. 2 (2006): 278–284.

33. National Institutes of Health, "Kegel Exercises," *Medline Plus Medical Encyclopedia*, http://www.nlm.nih.gov/medlineplus/ency/article/003975.htm (accessed August 8, 2005).

34. Schwartz and Andrasik, 464.

35. National Institute of Neurological Disorders and Stroke, "Epilepsy Information Page," http://www.ninds.nih.gov/disorders/epilepsy/epilepsy.htm (accessed July 17, 2006).

36. Neumann and Birbaumer, 78–83.

37. U. Kraft, "Train Your Brain," *Scientific American Mind* 17, no. 1 (2006): 58–63.

38. Wrong Diagnosis, "Statistics by Country for Paralysis," http://www.wrongdiagnosis.com/p/paralysis/stats-country.htm (accessed December 5, 2006).

39. Neumann and Birbaumer, 78–83.

40. Mayo Clinic, "Biofeedback: Using Your Mind to Improve Your Health," *Complementary and Alternative Medicine,* http://www.mayoclinic.com/health/biofeedback/SA00083 (accessed December 5, 2006).

41. Ibid.

42. Department of Health and Human Services, "Medicare Coverage of Urinary Incontinence Therapies," *Centers for Medicare and Medicaid Services,* http://www.cms.hhs.gov/apps/media/press/release.asp?Counter=386 (accessed December 5, 2006).

43. Mayo Clinic, "Biofeedback: Using Your Mind to Improve Your Health."

44. National Center for Complementary and Alternative Medicine, "Treatment of Therapy," http://nccam.nih.gov/health/bytreatment.htm (accessed July 11, 2006).

45. Centers for Disease Control, "Complementary and Alternative Medicine Use Among Adults: United States, 2002," *Advance Date from Vital and Health Statistics*, http://www.cdc.gov/nchs/data/ad/ad343.pdf (accessed December 5, 2006).

46. Ian Parker, "Reading Minds," *The New Yorker Magazine* 78, no. 43 (2003): 52–63.

47. Tom Collura, in e-mail to author, July 20, 2006.

48. Ibid.

49. Ibid.

50. Schwartz and Andrasik, 905–907.

51. Ibid., 894.

52. Ibid., 895.

53. Ibid., 893.

Glossary

Abdomen The space between the chest and the hips.

Antidepressant A drug that affects how chemical substances act in the brain; the traditional treatment for severe depression.

Asthma A long-term disease that causes irritated, obstructed airways in the lungs.

Attention Deficit Hyperactivity Disorder (ADHD) A disorder that affects a person's ability to concentrate; a common mental disorder in children.

Biofeedback A method that uses instruments to make information about the body available to the mind.

Brain A collection of 100 billion nerve cells that acts as the control center for the entire human body.

Brain waves The electrical signals produced by nerve cells in the brain.

Cancer A group of disorders in which the cells in the body multiply uncontrollably and invade other parts of the body.

Central nervous system The brain and the spinal cord.

Controlled study A study in which there are two (or more) groups of subjects being followed, each of which lives in near identical conditions except for the treatment being tested.

Depression A state of extreme sadness or despair that disrupts an individual's daily life.

Electroencephalograph (EEG) A machine that detects electric signals in the brain and displays them on a monitor as brain waves.

Electromyograph (EMG) A machine that detects muscle movements and displays them on a monitor.

Epilepsy A brain disorder in which clusters of nerve cells send unusual electrical signals to the body.

Feedback A learning process in which signals are interpreted to determine future actions.

Finger phototransmitter A small sensor that clips softly to a patient's fingertip and uses light to measure vasoconstriction.

Galvanic skin response monitor (GSR) An instrument that indicates how much a person is sweating by measuring how much electricity can pass through the skin.

Heart rate variability (HRV) A measure of heart rate patterns over time.

Herpes A viral disease that can cause painful blisters on the mouth, lips, or genitals.

Hot flashes Short periods of heavy sweating, either at night or during the day, that occur during menopause in women.

Immune system The complex network of cells designed to respond to invading organisms in the body.

Incontinence The involuntary excretion of urine through the urethra or involuntary bowel movements through the anus.

Insomnia The inability to sleep for a long period of time.

Neurons Nerve cells.

Nervous system The brain, the spinal cord, and nerves that regulate and control how different parts of the body communicate with each other; includes the central nervous system and the peripheral nervous system.

Paralysis A complete loss of muscle movement in one or more locations in the body.

Peripheral nervous system The nerves in the body located outside of the brain and spinal cord.

Polygraph A device that measures response in the body, sometimes called a lie detector.

Relaxation The opposite of stress; it is often described as feeling "loose" and "comfortable."

Seizures Short periods of time when the brain is sending many strong electrical signals that can result in uncontrollable bodily movements.

Slow cortical potential (SCP) A positive or negative change in certain types of brain waves.

Stimulant A drug that increases activity in a particular part of the nervous system and makes a user feel more awake and alert.

Stress Something physical or behavioral that causes tension in the mind and body.

Substance addiction The repeated use of something, such as cigarettes or alcohol, to the point where the person is dependent on that substance.

Synapse The place where neurons communicate with other neurons.

Telehealth Computer and information technology used to educate and treat patients.

Thermometer A simple instrument that measures temperature.

Thought translation device A computer controlled by a person's slow cortical potential (SCP) brain waves.

Writer's cramp Muscle spasms caused when a person starts to write; caused by excess gripping or releasing of the pen or pencil.

Bibliography

Association for Applied Psychophysiology and Biofeedback, http://www.
aapb.org/ (accessed November 30, 2006).

Biofeedback Certification Institute of America, http://www.bcia.org/
(accessed November 30, 2006).

Biofeedback Newsmagazine, Association for Applied Psychophysiology and
Biofeedback, http://www.aapb.org/i4a/pages/Index.cfm?pageid=3538
(accessed November 30, 2006).

Morgan, Jennifer R., and Ona Bloom. *Cells of the Nervous System.*
New York: Chelsea House Publishing, 2006.

Neumann, Nicola, and Niels Birbaumer. "Thinking Out Loud." *Scientific
American Mind* 14 no. 5 (2004): 78–83.

Robbins, Tim. *A Symphony in the Brain.* New York: Grove Press, 2000.

Schwartz, Mark S., and Frank Andrasik. *Biofeedback: A Practitioner's
Guide.* New York: Guilford Press, 2003.

Sherman, Richard. *Pain: Assessment and Intervention.* Wheat
Ridge, Colo.: Association for Applied Psychophysiology and
Biofeedback, 2004.

Further Reading

Cefrey, Holly. *Antidepressants.* The Drug Abuse Prevention Library. New York: Rosen Publishing, 2000.

Cleveland, Donald. *How Do We Know How the Brain Works.* Great Scientific Questions and the Scientists Who Answered Them. New York: Rosen Publishing, 2005.

Crist, James J., Eric Braun, Catherine Broberg, Michael Chesworth. *What to Do When You're Sad & Lonely: A Guide for Kids.* Minneapolis, Minn: Free Spirit Publishing, 2006.

Morgan, Jennifer R., and Ona Bloom. *Cells of the Nervous System.* New York: Chelsea House Publishing, 2006.

Parker, Ian. "Reading Minds." *The New Yorker Magazine* 78, no. 43 (2003): 52–63.

Robbins, Tim. *A Symphony in the Brain.* New York: Grove Press, 2000.

Schwartz, Mark S., and Frank Andrasik. *Biofeedback: A Practitioner's Guide.* New York: Guilford Press, 2003.

Stroebel, Elizabeth. *Kiddie QR: A Choice for Children and Families.* Barrington, R.I.: self-published, 2006.

Web Sites

Association for Applied Psychophysiology and Biofeedback (AAPB)
http://www.aapb.org
A nonprofit organization whose goal is to "promote a new understanding of biofeedback and advance the methods used in this practice."

Biofeedback Certification Institute of America (BCIA)
http://www.bcia.org
The BCIA certifies qualified clinical health care workers to administer biofeedback treatments.

National Institutes of Health (NIH)
http://www.nih.gov
An organization funded by the government to conduct and support medical research.

National Mental Health Association (NMHA)
http://www.nmha.org
A nonprofit organization addressing mental health and mental illness issues through research, advocacy, education, and service.

10: © 2007 JupiterImages Corporation

11: © Martin Dohrn/Photo Researchers, Inc.

12: Infobase Publishing

17: Copyright © (2005) Applied Psychophysiology & Biofeedback. From Biofeedback. Reprinted by permission of Alliance Communications Group, a division of Allen Press, Inc.

23: Infobase Publishing

25: Infobase Publishing

27: Infobase Publishing

31: Courtesy of Dr. Tim Lowenstein

34: Courtesy of www.thoughttechnology.com

35: Infobase Publishing

37: © Phanie/ Photo Researchers, Inc.

39: Infobase Publishing

46: © Tracy Dominey/Photo Researchers, Inc.

55: Infobase Publishing

61: Infobase Publishing

64: © Dung Vo Trung/CORBIS SYGMA

66: ASSOCIATED PRESS

70: © Royalty-Free/CORBIS

78: © Scientifica/Visuals Unlimited

Index

About the Author

Krista West has two, seemingly unrelated, academic passions: biology and writing. A longtime lover of nature and wildlife, she earned a zoology degree from the University of Washington in Seattle. In graduate school, she pursued her love of writing and earned master's degrees in earth science and journalism at Columbia University in New York. Ms. West has been writing about science for newspapers, magazines, and book publishers for more than 10 years.

About the Editor

Eric H. Chudler, Ph.D., is a research neuroscientist who has investigated the brain mechanisms of pain and nociception since 1978. He is currently a research associate professor in the University of Washington Department of Bioengineering and director of education and outreach at University of Washington Engineered Biomaterials. Dr. Chudler's research interests focus on how areas of the central nervous system (cerebral cortex and basal ganglia) process information related to pain. He has also worked with other neuroscientists and teachers to develop educational materials to help students learn about the brain.